Time on Your Hands

A Study in Palmistry

Maiya Gray-Cobb

D1611754

4880 Lower Valley Road • Atglen, PA • 19310

Printed in the U.S.A.

ST. JOHN THE BAPTIST PARISH LIBRARY
2920 NEW HIGHWAY 51
LAPLACE, LOUISIANA 70068

Other Schiffer Books on Related Subjects:

Twist Your Fate Geof Gray-Cobb
ISBN 978-0-7643-2962-3, $14.99

Copyright © 2011 by Maiya Gray-Cobb
Library of Congress Control Number: 2011934273

Designed by Danielle D. Farmer
Cover Design by Bruce Waters
Type set in LtUnivers/Mistral/NewBskvll BT

ISBN: 978-0-7643-3904-2
Printed in the United States

Schiffer Books are available at special discounts for bulk purchases for sales promotions or premiums. Special editions, including personalized covers, corporate imprints, and excerpts can be created in large quantities for special needs. For more information contact the publisher:

Published by Schiffer Publishing Ltd.
4880 Lower Valley Road
Atglen, PA 19310
Phone: (610) 593-1777; Fax: (610) 593-2002
E-mail: Info@schifferbooks.com

For the largest selection of fine reference books on this and related subjects, please visit our website at **www.schifferbooks.com**
We are always looking for people to write books on new and related subjects. If you have an idea for a book, please contact us at **proposals@schifferbooks.com**

This book may be purchased from the publisher.
Include $5.00 for shipping.
Please try your bookstore first.
You may write for a free catalog.

In Europe, Schiffer books are distributed by
Bushwood Books
6 Marksbury Ave.
Kew Gardens
Surrey TW9 4JF England
Phone: 44 (0) 20 8392 8585; Fax: 44 (0) 20 8392 9876
E-mail: info@bushwoodbooks.co.uk
Website: www.bushwoodbooks.co.uk

Dedication

For my husband, Geof, for all the years we shared together. Passed on in May 2009, now always in my memory.

Also for my two closest and helpful friends, Colleen and Laura.

Contents

Figure 1:
Major and Minor Lines

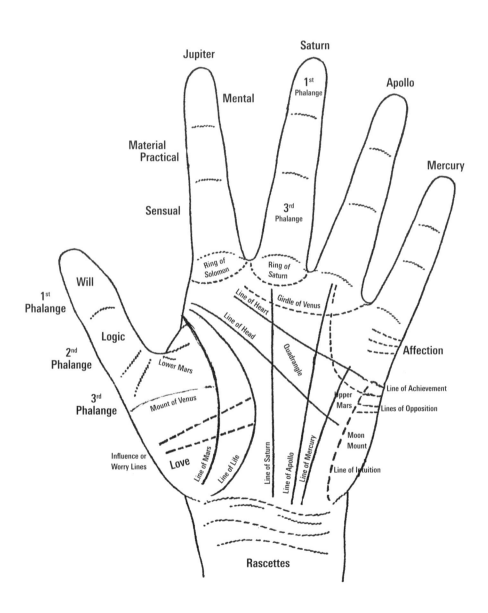

Jupiter

Saturn

Apollo

Mercury

Mental

1st Phalange

3rd Phalange

Material Practical

Sensual

Ring of Solomon

Ring of Saturn

Girdle of Venus

Will

1st Phalange

Line of Heart

Line of Head

Logic

2nd Phalange

Lower Mars

Quadrangle

Affection

3rd Phalange

Mount of Venus

Upper Mars

Line of Achievement

Lines of Opposition

Moon Mount

Influence or Worry Lines

Love

Line of Mars

Line of Life

Line of Saturn

Line of Apollo

Line of Mercury

Line of Intuition

Rascettes

Foreword

We always love to know something about ourselves. Whoever said "curiosity killed the cat" is dead wrong! Indeed we do have a need to know who we really are and there is no one as curious as ourselves when the "need to know" bug bites us.

Have you noticed that whenever there is a personality quiz, an IQ test, or a psychological assessment in a magazine or book we instinctively reach for a pencil to fill in the blanks?

How about the astrology column in the newspaper that we turn to first to help us through the day? Then, of course, there is the astrology year book to take us through the whole year, even if it does talk about only the sun signs. Nevertheless, something in your sun sign always clicks and you get a kick out of reading all those little quirks you hadn't really thought about.

Somehow, it gives us a tremendous sense of fulfillment to know more about ourselves. This makes us feel a lot better, as it pumps up our ego for a while and helps to satisfy some of our curiosity.

From time immemorial, the lure of the unknown and hidden things has always held a fascination for us. The human mind just simply has "to know," whether it is investigating the past, the present, or the future.

There are many fascinating psychic and occult sciences that are worthy of consideration – tea leaf reading for instance. My husband, Geof Gray-Cobb, had one many years ago by the mother of an acquaintance. We really didn't believe in that sort of thing then, but she told him he would become a very successful writer (he was a scientist, working for NASA in South Africa at that time). He would also become quite famous on TV some time after we had moved to another country ending in an "A." We laughed about it and didn't take it seriously – particularly when you think of all the countries ending in an "A." Interestingly, it came to pass. NASA closed the tracking station and we moved from South Africa to Canada where many of you know how famous he actually did become and what a successful writer he was. I speak in the past tense as he passed away in May of 2009.

There are other subjects that bear looking into, bringing satisfaction to curious minds. The I Ching for instance, the Chinese Book of

Changes. Then numerology, which is quite an eye opener, tarot cards with their symbology opening up the subconscious mind, and graphology, now classed as being scientific, frequently used in police investigations by specially trained document examiners looking into cases of fraud and forgery. These examiners also use handwriting analysis on letters and documents, especially historical papers/letters/signatures to attest to their authenticity.

The most interesting of all is palmistry as it has such tremendous depth. Again, this subject has been allocated to scientific use in police and detective work using the whorls on the finger tips. We all have distinctive finger tips belonging only to ourselves.

Right now, just take a brief look at the lines on the palms of your hands, and believe it or not, these indicate the moment of your birth to the time you pass from this life.

These tell you the story of your past, present, and future, indicating your character traits, natural inclinations and abilities, how you have used them in the development of your life, and the way you can use them in your future endeavors.

Has your curiosity been stimulated to seek further inside yourself? Then here is a book that will keep your ego on track. It will intrigue and challenge you from the first page, then reward you with the greatest assessment of yourself that you've ever had.

Why? Because you have done it all yourself and you have now discovered that:

THIS
IS YOUR
LIFE!

Acknowledgments

Where would I be without such a creative, helpful, and patient editor, who took time to answer all my questions and queries. Thank you Dinah Roseberry for the tremendous amount of work you and your design team have done to turn my words into such a beautiful book.

Your Hands are Your Own Book of Fate

Chapter 1

Again briefly, to further your interest:

Elementary

No 1. The Elementary type hand is frequently a thick, coarse, heavy hand with short fingers, its owner being the earthy type with a great deal of common sense.

Spatulate

No 2. The Spatulate type hand is usually large and broad with thick blunt fingers, shaped like a spade and thick at the tips. Here is an active person with much originality.

Conical

No 3. The Conical type, has a rounded base to the hand, round fingers which taper and the thumb often bends outwards. This one is usually a temperamental person.

Square

No 4. The Square type is unmistakably a square shape, also describing its owner as such. The palm is usually as wide as it is long and the fingers are frequently squarish.

Pointed

No 5. The Pointed type, often called the psychic hand, invariably more idealistic than psychic, is delicate and graceful, as are the owners. The fingertips are also pointed.

Knotty or Philosophic

No 6. The Knotty or Philosophic type is generally long, angular, with bony fingers and long nails. This is the hand of the analyst, the deep thinker, quite possibly of a mystical nature.

Mixed

No 7. The Mixed type contains some of the characteristics of the previous six types of hand. With a mixture of this and that of the above we find a versatile person and the hand can be any shape or size.

There are many other factors involved in reading the palms which will modify these general characteristics – the basic assessment – which you first make. It is somewhat similar to developing an astrological chart. Once the chart is mathematically erected, the general characteristics are shown by a combination of the Sun, Moon, and the Ascendant, their rulers and the houses the rulers occupy. When the aspects are taken out and applied to this information and also to the various sections of life, then the whole picture of the person comes alive.

So it is with a palmistry reading. Once the general indications are dealt with – the thumb and the shape of the hand – the length of the fingers give hints of adjustment. Then again, are the fingers smooth or knotty? Is the hand soft, hard or flabby depicting the physical energy? What do the major lines have to say and also the secondary lines which point to love, marriage, health, and spirituality? The mounts of the fingers will be the final arbiters.

It is also most interesting to note that the mounts – seven of them – are named after the seven inner planets and that they have the same attributes applied to the hand as is applied to an astrology chart. The four elements of astrology, Fire, Earth, Air, and Water show up as elemental combinations within a hand altering the degree of qualities. No hand belongs exclusively to one pure type. All are open to refinement.

In a nutshell, we have here the basis of your hands as a whole. The left hand being the subjective hand shows what traits and talents you are born with – your inherited background. The right hand tells what you have done or can do with them. You can see this quite plainly by the changes that have taken place in the lines on the right hand when you have applied your own specific individuality to that particular area of your life. So which hand are you going to read? Both actually, for each contains the necessary information which, when put together, shows *you* as the whole person you are now and how you got there – your own personal path in life.

Establish first then which is your dominant – major – hand, the one you mostly use for writing, using tools, picking up things, waving, pointing your fingers. You will, of course, be consulting both hands at different times, noting the difference between the lines of each. The minor hand indicates what you hope to get out of life, the major hand shows what you have brought into it by grasping opportunities or letting them slip by and also how you cope with the setbacks which we all run into at one time or another.

The minor hand shows your feelings and emotions, your uncertainties and anxieties, and the dominant hand shows more of the practical side of life. In studying this dominant hand you can gather information about your career, money, travel, and how you adapt to changes in your life. Looking at the minor one you'll find information about your love life, marriage, children, and the personal things in life that interest you. So always read both hands – what you can't find in one you will find in the other.

Important Instruction:

One final word before we move to the next chapter: If you happen to be left handed, the right hand will become the subjective (minor) hand and the left hand the dominant one, so all the details in this book should be applied in reverse.

Thumbs Up

Chapter 2

Figure 2:
Thumbs

Large thumb

3 positions
high, normal, low set

**Small thumb on small
pointed hand**

Waisted thumb

Thick thumb

Short clubbed thumb

**Short thumb
and bent fingers**

Long slender thumb

I've considered the shape of the hand, the thumbs and this and that in deciding where to start within this infinite array of information contained in the hands. Most palmistry books start with the shape of the hand but I asked myself this question: Does the hand hinge on the thumb or does the thumb hinge on the hand? In either case, the traits, qualities, strength, or weakness of character described by the type of the thumb are usually the same as the type of the hand to which it belongs. As the thumb is really the key to character, I decided to lead off with this digit, it being the most important to the hand. It is a most valuable organ. Just think about how you grasp a drinking glass, a door knob, a pen or pencil, a bottle top, hold tools, turn a tap on or off (and I tried that one on the tap this morning), and a variety of other things. Without it, life becomes so much more of a challenge as all the fingers revolve around the grip of the thumb.

The thumb speaks volumes as we shall see. In fact, it is such a great revealer of character, so great, that by simply looking at the length, set, angle, size and shape, it can tell you a tremendous amount about its owner without even going any further. After that we will investigate the three phalanges and the "three worlds" then you will be amazed at what the thumb has told you about your character and your friends and family if you take a quick look at them.

The Length of the Thumb

Point One

So the first point in examining the thumb is its length. To find this, first hold your hand, palm towards you. Now lay your thumb, loosely, upright against and close to the first finger (that's known as the Jupiter finger) The normal length of the thumb is where the tip reaches round about the middle of the third phalange of the first finger –that's the bottom bit of the finger that joins the palm. If the thumb goes above this (into the second phalange – that's the middle bit) this is a long thumb. If it is situated well down in the third phalange, it is a short thumb. Another way to check the length is to align the thumb of one hand against the little finger (the Mercury finger) of the other hand. They should be the same length indicating a normal length of thumb. So what does this little bit of information tell you about yourself or other people?

A long thumb is indicative of an intelligent nature. There is strength of character here, ruled more by the head than by the heart and the personality leans more towards diplomacy. Long thumb folks try much harder to get what they want.

With a short thumb you'll find the day-dreamers of this world. These people are talkers not doers. They use less reasoning ability, lack will power and are frequently guided by their emotions.

A very short thumb – mental disabilities are frequently shown by a shorter thumb, and one that is poorly developed often shows a lack of control over passions and emotions. If it is particularly stiff and unyielding when the top joint is pressed there may well be a hot temper.

Point Two

Now the second point is: What is the set of the thumb, high or low, what is its angle and what size is it?

Does the thumb lie close to the side of the hand with just a small gap in between? This is called a high set thumb. It indicates a person who is probably careful with money and not particularly generous. This high set thumb shows a mostly cautious nature, having a secretive side, keeping others at arms length. They rarely make friends nor do they wish to do so for fear of others taking advantage of them or asking favors of them. If the top joint is stiff and unyielding when it is pressed there are likely to be deep down fears left over from childhood. Here you may also find a person who is stubborn, and determined with somewhat narrow views and morals.

If the top joint bends backwards slightly there will be more flexibility within the nature, and a looser thumb, standing away from the hand with a supple joint, indicates one who is generous, broad-minded, and tolerant of others. Generally being good humored there will be no problem in readily adapting to different circumstances.

Point Three

Number 3: If the thumb is placed low on the hand, especially with a wide angle between the base of the thumb and the first (Jupiter) finger there is a tendency to be rather careless and irresponsible, yet generous and compassionate in nature. Very independent, this person has a love of liberty. Now if the angle of the thumb is too wide – far removed from the first finger and tending to lean outwards, there is a demand for total freedom of action. There is a disregard for other people, a great deal of selfishness and a likelihood of being anti-social.

If the thumb is really set well down (somewhat like a chimpanzee), it shows a lack of intellect and the owner of this thumb is more inclined towards the sensual and material matters of life. If this low set thumb is very long and occasionally it is, it will add power and force to the character, and the length of the phalanges may also add determination and reason revealing the driving force that gives motivation.

Point Four

Next: number 4. What size is the thumb? This indicates your basic energy, how you utilize it – in other words, where and how you put it into action. The strength or weakness shown in the size of the thumb points to the strength or absence of the same in the character of its owner. So is the thumb large or small?

Large thumbs invariably show a strong character, frequently guided by the head rather than the heart and emotions. It is a capable thumb belonging to a forceful personality, usually a natural ruler, especially if the thumb feels coarse when stroked. These large thumb people enjoy and seek out useful, practical things. They are generally more motivated, ambitious and persistent than other people, therefore they are more inclined to reach their goals or achieve the top positions they are aiming for. Interestingly, these large thumb people frequently have a love of history.

In contrast, small thumbs tend to have a weak or weaker character, due to being guided by their heart and sentiments. They lack the motivation and ambition of the large thumb folk, neither do they have the force to be pushy and expose themselves to the rigors of life. Other people take advantage of them, and their lives are often guided by others. They have a romantic nature, appreciating the beautiful, poetical and sentimental side of life. They also have a strong dislike of challenges.

Point Five

Finally we will look at the shape of the thumb before we discuss the phalanges and the three worlds that show how the combined qualities, traits, and energy are being used.

In the previous chapter, I mentioned the types of hands and you will find that the shape of the thumb invariably corresponds to the shape (type) of the hand, and the shape of both thumb and hand affects the attitude towards life as you will see within the next chapter.

Take a good look at the thumb: Is it tapered in the middle? This is often called a "waisted" thumb – shaped like a persons waist. This shows intelligence, a well-balanced mind and a tactful, diplomatic nature. If there is excessive waisting, which usually occurs just below where the thumb bends forward, (on the second phalange) there is much tact and diplomacy but also a great deal of cunning. Avoid doing business with these thumb people, you'll get shafted as they cannot really be trusted.

A straight up thumb with no shape at all to it shows a lack of tact. Argumentative to extremes, reasoning power will be used to make a point whether right or wrong.

If it is a thick thumb, there's a very definite stubborn streak here, once this person's mind is made up it's hard to change it.

Extremely thick thumbs invariably indicate violent tendencies, tread warily with these folk.

Slender thumbs belong to the patient and tolerant people of this world, and quite frequently, there is artistic genius hidden within.

Now there is one more shape of thumb that is called the "Clubbed" thumb. It will be set very low on the hand, short, and thick in the second portion of the thumb, (the second phalange) and the upper portion will be very short, broad, thick and heavy with a short, flat nail. This is often called the "murderers" thumb, but this doesn't mean that murder will always be committed – there have to be particular circumstances for this to take place. But there will undoubtedly be uncontrolled passion, invariably over-ruling any reason that they may have. If the first joint is extremely stiff, there will be a remarkable obstinacy of purpose. When the temper is out of control the subject can easily be driven towards violence and crime but even then, other circumstances will be involved.

The Three Phalanges of the Thumb

Before we move on to the next chapter of the shapes of hands we will investigate the three phalanges of the thumb. The first phalange (the top portion inside the thumb) represents will power, the determination to achieve a particular desire and also the ability to command others. The second phalange (in the middle of the thumb) indicates reason and logic, i.e., perception (being aware of something through one of the five senses) the ability to judge what you perceive and then to make decisions. The third phalange involves love, sentiment, sympathy, and passion, situated at the base of the thumb on what is called the Mount of Venus. This mount we will discuss elsewhere in greater detail when we come to the interesting Mounts. This will tie much information together.

As I mentioned before, the thumb is the driving force that motivates us all and the qualities and quantities of energy that are shown within the thumb describe how we use them – how we direct them towards the external world. This is how we determine our own life style.

Length of the Phalanges

Ideally, the top two phalanges should be the same length, but there are usually differences between them. If they are the same length, you will note that there is an equal amount of logic and willpower being used on a daily basis. These people come up with very good ideas and they also have the necessary drive and energy to put them successfully into action. In other words this combination of phalanges shows how they tend to arrange their own life style. For instance, their lives will be well organized, quite possibly in a ritualistic manner – the sort of people others describe as "you can set the clock by them." Other lengths of phalanges will indicate something entirely different.

Just as we did earlier with the thumb, we shall now look at the length, the size, and the shape of each phalange, to see the quality and quantity hidden within.

Look inside the thumb, bend it slightly and you will see the two phalanges. If the top (first) phalange is *very* long and the second tends to be short, there is a recklessness here in both thought and action. There is very little reasoning behind the actions, no control over the willpower and not much common sense. With some people there is a tendency towards despotism and an uncontrolled temper, the shape of both thumb and hand combined will indicate if this is part of the nature.

Now, if there is a *very short* first phalange and a long second, these are the talkers. They are all talk and very little "do." They have good strong reasoning power but poor execution. There is a lack of drive to carry out the task.

If the first phalange is longer than the second, there's a strong and healthy willpower occasionally overriding logic. They can be highly stubborn, sometimes inflexible, but there is also great determination to reach a desired goal. They are likely, through their stubbornness, to make plenty of mistakes, but they'll start again and carry on until they have reached their goal. They can also be rather domineering.

But if the second phalange is the longer, what a lot of ideas there are, yet somehow they never seem to be put into action. Thought is a fine thing, but without the motivation to act, these people will just continue to think about them. If that second phalange is very long, there is clever reasoning yet a great lack of will power. Little action takes place when they are left to their own devices, things are started, incentive fails and not much is completed. These people will bore you right out of your mind discussing everything under the sun, trying to make an impression, even if they don't really know much about the subject.

A short first phalange frequently indicates a lack of self control, and a very short second, signifies weak willpower, weak reasoning used in fits and starts, and a tendency to be obstinate, careless and silly.

Just as the first phalange pointed to the strength of will and the power of endurance, the second phalange gave more information regarding the nature and temperament. Each action that is taken is guided by logic, so if willpower is required to carry out a task, logic will be utilized to think and to plan out the actions. What can alter these indications? The shape of the tip of the thumb.

Study the tip now. Is the tip Conical in shape (this means rounded and pointed) and long? Here you will find artistic gifts, but if it is short there will be laziness, lots of imaginings and inconstancy. In the previous chapter, I mentioned that a Conical type of hand indicated a temperamental person, now add that to these artistic gifts and you'll often find that artistic people are somewhat temperamental. See how things are beginning to fit together?

If the tip of the thumb is narrow and pointed this shows plenty of energy yet it is constantly being used up in a scattered way. Making a decision is frequently difficult because there is little staying power. Procrastination takes over much of the time so the quality of this energy fluctuates leading to poor quantity.

If the thumb tip is completely pointed, this indicates a great deal of creativity combined with an exceptional amount of intelligence.

When the tip of the thumb is rounded without the point, these people usually get on well with others. If necessary, they can be quite authoritative, and they will quickly spring to the defense of weaker people.

A long square tip indicates much will power and they will always play the game of life with a love of fair play. They are also very practical, but if it happens to be a short square tip there is a great deal of indecision, a constant change of mind, and total disinterest in what is going on around them.

The Spatulate tip if it is long, shows a strong will, strategically used, frequently indicating a craftsperson, but if it is short, there is a hesitation in making decisions at the right time which frequently leaves other people in the lurch.

The thumb with a wedge-shaped tip tells you that these people know very well what they want and they will continue on until they get it. They are very determined but will negotiate if absolutely necessary.

The thick straight tip sees everything in black and white. There are no shades of gray; there is nothing in between as far as they are concerned. Don't even think about negotiating – to them, the word does not exist! But if the thumb tip is shaped like a waist, even if it is thick, there is more flexibility.

A thin tip shows one who is weak in will and very possibly in health as well. And a thick thumb with no shape marks a lascivious disposition often accompanied by violence.

Now the broad thumbed tip indicates a person who is a very obstinate creature, and if the tip is long there is a good understanding of material things. If the tip tends to be short, they will want their material things and will be constantly fretful until they get them.

On the contrary, the thumb with a slender tip belongs to one who is refined, and likes to be seen as such. This person is courteous in every way, especially towards achieving success. Don't be fooled here, this is the iron hand in a velvet glove.

With the flat-tipped thumb there is an insignificant and nervous personality, hidden quite well and coming across as a gentle person. There is a lack of both energy and logic here, and the owner of this thumb tends to hide behind the facade of wanting to be thought of as "refined" but is very capable of nagging until their wants are satisfied.

The Three Worlds

Now to the "three worlds" indicated by the thumb, the tip and the phalanges.

We can see that the first "world" is of the mind – how you use your thinking patterns to help you to adjust and adapt yourself to the circumstances that life brings to you.

The second "world" shows how practical you are and how you put your ideas into action.

The third "world" indicates your physical needs and how you go about achieving them in combination with the two previous "worlds" of intellect and logic.

With all the interesting facts you've just worked through you have now been able to discern a great deal about your own character. Is it strong or weak? Do you see yourself as being Intellectual or logical and practical? Are you gentle or aggressive? How about creative or just plain humdrum? Whatever you think you are at this moment, let's now turn to chapter three and look at the variety of shapes of hands which could well alter the opinion you now have of yourself.

Hand Shapes

—

What Type Are You?

Chapter 3

Figure 3:
Types of Hands

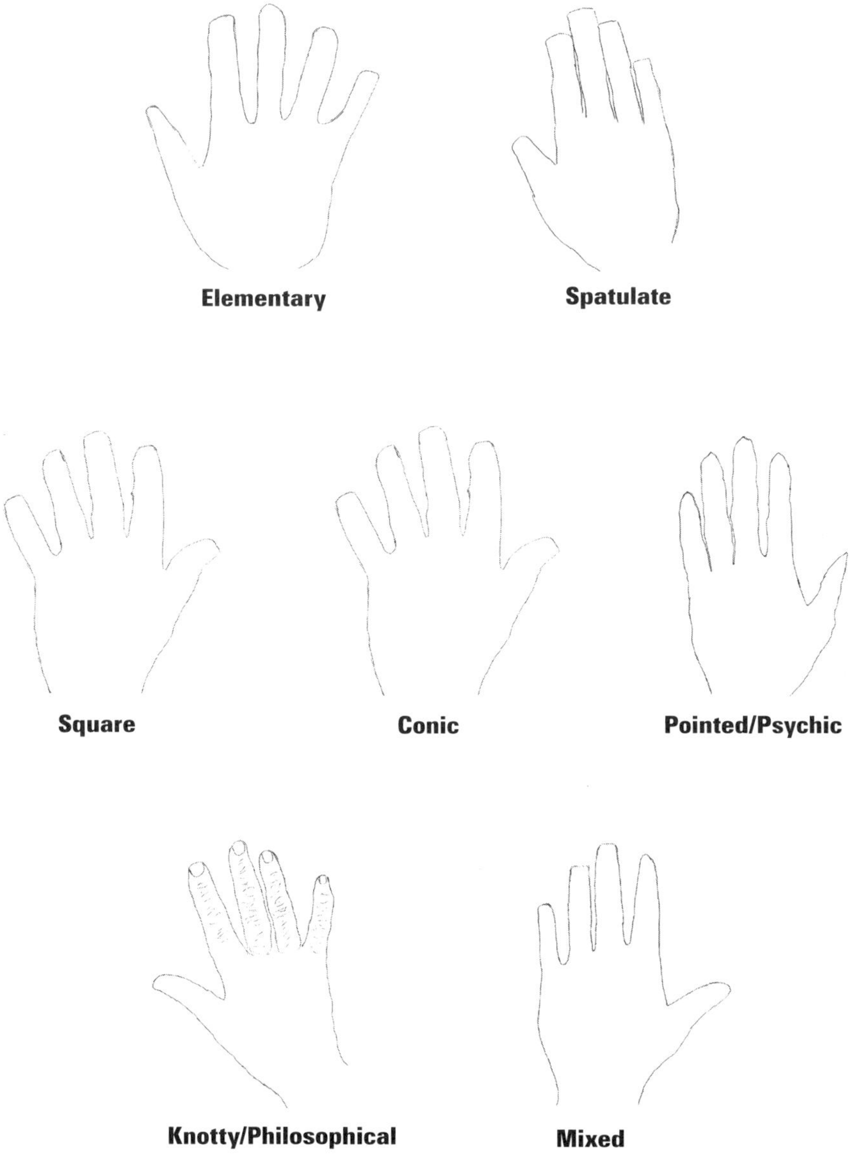

Elementary

Spatulate

Square

Conic

Pointed/Psychic

Knotty/Philosophical

Mixed

Chapter by chapter you'll find the information relating to your hands, and the secrets contained within become more and more interesting. Seeing yourself developing from your past through your sub-dominant hand then into your present status is quite a fascinating procedure. As you learn to read the lines and mounts of the fingers in later chapters you'll be able to develop a view of your future. Of course, you are anxious to know your love life, whether you'll be successful in business, earn or marry a lot of money, or what type of job you are suited for.

Part of the answers to those questions are contained within the next five chapters which we are about to investigate, starting with the shape of the hand. The shape really is important along with the shape and length of the fingers and their phalanges and some other things that we will cover later.

Here's an example. For instance: You want to know about money in your life – a most necessary commodity. Now, are you going to inherit it, win it in a lottery, marry it or work for it? If it is the latter, are you sufficiently ambitious and goal oriented to go after it, putting your whole self into it above everything else to acquire a millionaire status? Then you need to have strong, blunt fingers and a thick strong type of hand that indicates material motivation and good organizing ability, preferably the Spatulate hand.

Now, after studying the chapters that are coming up, you discover you have these indications, look back at your notes on the thumb set from Chapter Two. Do they show that your thumb is held close to the hand? Greed and secretiveness is shown here, but a little flexibility of the top joint alters some of the greedy nature and more of an openness towards differing circumstances. What of the other notes you have there? Apply and integrate them with the type of hand you have discovered for yourself. Once again, you can see how some of chapter two will fit with the upcoming chapters to round out your personality and the quality and quantity of your strengths and weaknesses.

On the other hand, I know you will want to flip towards the end of the book to see if you will win a lottery. Go ahead and your question will be answered if you can see or find a cross or more than one on the Mount of Apollo. But where is the Mount of Apollo? Take a sneak peek at chapter ten!

So for a start, lets find out what type you are.

Palmistry was established upon the shape of the hand indicating the type of person you are. This is where all your traits and qualities show up. Now, as you are well aware, your hand carries out all the work you do when it receives an order from your brain which is actually the hand's dominating power. Your hand mirrors the type of brain that you have inherited and its characteristics can be seen by the manner and intelligence with which your actions are carried out.

As I mentioned briefly in Chapter One, there are seven types (shapes) of hands, all indicating different types of mentality. Remember that what you define here can be altered to a great extent by the lines and particularly the mounts of the fingers. What we are looking at right now are just the general indications. Note them down as you go along and later they can be added to or subtracted as you put the whole picture together. Now we will examine the hands in more detail.

Hand Number 1 – Elementary

Number 1 is the Elementary hand, usually pointing to the dullness of personality. It is a large hand, somewhat coarse, not very flexible and the fingers are nearly always short and thick. This type of hand has been inherited down the ages from ancestors who lived hard and tough lives. Naturally, their self preservation and acquisitive faculties became well developed.

The dullness of character here is reflected in being a "down to earth person," having little interest in things of an intellectual nature or of a fine quality like art, music, poetry, and other natural beauties that make the soul sing.

This is the hand of the farmer, bricklayer, road worker, garbage collector, one who has a practical, industrious, shrewd nature. This hand shows an inclination towards being rather coarse, jealous, covetous, and cunning, hovering between truth and lies whenever necessary

Many male children with this hand have been influenced by one parent, usually the father or grandfather, who is stern, unbending, knows what is right for the family and is quick to use a strap or belt to keep them in line. From this upbringing, a hot-tempered passionate nature has developed. Frequently, a strong religious influence has been enforced which has endowed the child with a violence and a lust for killing in the name of "God," especially if other people's religious and political philosophies appear to threaten their own. This will be emphasized if the line of Mars which lies just inside the Life line, branches across the palm to end in the Mount of Moon (See the Figure 1). A combination of the emotions of the Moon and the quick temper of Mars brings out a brutal, intemperate nature and if the end of the line is forked it indicates an unstable person with a violent and vicious disposition. Although mostly superstitious, narrow minded, morally weak, and not especially intellectual, a number of great leaders with this particular elementary type of hand have arisen to carry out religious persecutions and their power and influence has shaped future events.

Now there is a secondary type of elementary hand that, over time, has drifted away from the hard farm type life and the influence of fanatically religious -struck parents. Qualities of the intellect have been developed through reading, further education, and the mental attitude of a definite desire to improve both lifestyle and to bring about changes. Change happens over a period of time – from generation to generation, through environment, life influences, intellectual, and spiritual development. The advent of television and the computer has had a great influence on the elementary hand/mind/brain and it is seen much today where young people no longer wish to use their hands but employ their minds instead. The lines and mounts in the dominant hand will show these changes and further achievements to be attained in the future through their own powers. If weaknesses are recognized, tackled, and conquered then life changes will most definitely happen.

This secondary type of hand is most interesting to investigate. All the attributes applied to the previous paragraph of this elementary hand still apply to this one but they are utilized in a different manner. The basic characteristics here are influenced by the mother, not the male side of the family. If she is of a gentle religious nature she can easily influence her children to enter the church, to worship a "loving God" as opposed to the bloodthirsty nature of the previous hand in the name of God. The Jupiter mount will show any influence here as far as religion is concerned.

A warmth and passion is exuded in other ways and it will be shown with a line from the Mount of Venus – the third phalange at the base of the thumb reaching up to the Mount of Jupiter that is just below the first finger. If Jupiter's mount is "puffy" it leans more towards religion and ambition. If the mount under the little (Mercury) finger is "puffy" the intellectual side will begin to be more developed and an urge to attend universities and gain degrees will be more in evidence.

Active, industrious, shrewd, and efficient, the owner of this hand can also influence or shape future events, but in a positive way. There is a certain egotism here that can turn into a dullness of character if overused, boring people who will turn away. If this happens, a docility – that will turn into a weakness, is likely to take over, leading eventually to jealousy and excessive greed, thereby falling into the original pattern of the hand previously described. This would be a pity as the growth of this hand is indicative of the development of a new soul starting out on its spiritual path.

Hand Number 2 – Spatulate

The Number 2 hand is the Spatulate type. It too, is large, broad with thick blunt fingers, widening slightly at the tips to resemble a spatula. The palm is often hard and unyielding rather than springy in texture. If this is the case, the owner will be hard hearted and difficult to handle, determined and fixed in purpose. Note that the hand spreads out in a sort of fan shape. There are two types of spatulate hands: one where the palm is wider at the wrist than at the base of the fingers, and the second type is reversed – being wider at the base of the fingers than at the wrist. Both types of hand indicate a great deal of activity, usually in most original ways.

They are very much attracted to and good at sports of all kinds. Some would like to choose it as a career, but check the strength of mind before making a decision. The top phalanges on the fingers point to mental strength and power. If the mind is not strong enough for total concentration and dedication, failure will take place. This could set up a syndrome of lack of self control, deliberately causing hurt or trouble for other people, and failing to carry out made promises. In this case, sports should be enjoyed as a pastime, an exercise, or passing on knowledge in the form of teaching/coaching; and then do something else as a career.

Career wise, they have interesting choices. Looking back in history, these hands point to navigators and explorers, discoverers of unknown lands, the courageous pioneers who have opened up and developed new lands for other people to make new lives for themselves. Others have been involved in opening up air routes, linking the Atlantic and Pacific by railway and opening the canals like the Suez and the Panama. Ingenious, indeed. In our modern world today, these are the folks who would love to be astronauts, to explore space and other planets and galaxies.

They are also attracted to science and engineering, ambitious and independent and preferring to work with their own ideas rather than other people's. They are very much individualists. Here is the inventor or mechanical genius, usually intolerant of convention being original in thought and action.

Surprisingly, some of our greatest painters and musicians have this spatulate shape of hand, but instead of the fingertips looking like little spades, cone shape tips, and other indications, theirs will show this artistic quality.

In the world of business, they can become successful executors or administrators and make good business partners. Many millionaires have this type of hand.

There's a great deal of change in the lives of people with a spatulate hand. They are interesting, adventurous people who love to travel. Although they are faithful working partners, they are not especially reliable as a life companion; neither are they interested in being tied down.

This would appear to be the next growth of the soul on its upward climb as this hand indicates a restless agitator who seeks to improve the lives of others through his/her own endeavors. If the base of the fingers is wider than the wrist, some of the characteristics of one or both parents will have been absorbed. If the parents are humanitarian by nature they will applaud and supply encouragement toward all his or her chosen endeavors. Further confirmation of this inherited disposition will also be reflected in the fingers, the shape of the finger nails and the texture of the skin.

Hand Number 3 – Conical

Number 3 is the Conical hand; it has a round base and a long palm that tapers slightly towards the top. The round fingers are full at the base, usually smooth, slightly pointed at the tips, with long nails that are often shaped like cones. The thumb is thick, unusually big and frequently bends outwards.

These are not easy people to get along with as they are generally ruled by their emotions. Impetuous and impulsive, they are exuberant at one moment, then quickly down in the dumps caused by trivial things. Theirs is a somewhat unstable nature whose temperament is colored by varying moods that change very quickly. Music and paintings stimulate their sensitivity, sometimes bringing on tears, for their aesthetic appreciation is strongly developed. If the fingers have any squareness to them they will usually be impressed by religious paintings. If the line of Head is quite straight in the palm down to the Mount of Luna, they are very capable themselves of creating religious paintings, otherwise they are likely to have little power to express their artistic ideas. If there is even a hint of squareness in the palm or the finger/tips this will add the ability to bring their creative ideas to fruition. In fact, a good point to remember in interpreting all palmistry is that any squareness, in any shape of hands, palms, or fingers tips will always add common sense and the ability to finish any chosen tasks.

As a general rule people with Conic hands are usually more influenced by artistic things than being artistic themselves as they are rather temperamental, sentimental, and romantic, clever and quick in thought and ideas, yet devoid of patience to carry out any of their intentions. They are also influenced by their surroundings and by the people they come in contact with. They sparkle beautifully in company, attracting either sex. Being good conversationalists they get the drift of subjects very quickly, but their knowledge is usually superficial.

This hand is very characteristic of the creative field – dancers, painters, sculptors, musicians, poets, actors, actresses, singers, writers. The emotional qualities mentioned above are needed to bring success to their endeavors, even if they read like negative traits. Imagine a very sensitive, emotional female singer who can lose herself in the character she is playing and move the audience to tears with her rendering. Actors, actresses, and all others I have mentioned – even writers who can make you cry over their books from the first page to the last – have this same ability and tend to live life on a sensual level. Everything with them is an emotional issue and they can most certainly be a pain to live with, particularly as they become offended easily. They judge by impulse and instinct, short tempered but it is over very quickly, but if they are really out of temper they will speak their minds very plainly.

This hand is often referred to as belonging to selfish people and some can be so, neglecting their family in favor of social life or where their own personal comfort is concerned. On the other hand, due to their sentimental nature they can be imposed upon when their sympathies are aroused. They are easily influenced to give money to charity, they give to anything or anybody as they have little power of discrimination and impulse takes over. Nevertheless, if they can be understood by partners, friends, and family, they are most interesting people as one never knows what is going to come next.

Hand Number 4 – Square

Number 4 is the Square hand, square at the wrist, square at the base of the fingers, and the fingers themselves are frequently square. Here we have the useful, practical people we find in so many walks of life. Orderly and punctual with a respect for discipline and authority, they like to have a personally ordered place for everything, and everything is kept in its place, in both household and brain. Law and Order could be their middle name!

The true square hand and square finger people are somewhat resistant to change, being creatures of habit. They are not usually quarrelsome, just determined in opposition when change appears on the horizon. With their forceful, determined, and tenacious nature, these methodical, matter of fact individuals are frequently very successful in their business matters. Their strong principles, honesty, sincerity, moral strength, and their rhythmic approach to life guarantees success in the professions of lawyer, teacher, politician, or even a member of the clergy, due to being a sturdy supporter of the existing order of things. Being practical by nature, they also have a love of the exact sciences plus an interest in agriculture and commerce.

They are not too intellectual or even enthusiastic over art, poetry, and the creative side of life but if there is a very obvious curve to the edge of the palm they will be creative in a practical and constructive way. Their businesslike attitude can accumulate wealth through their financial or technical ability. There are many jobs that interest this practical square type person if that creativity is shown on the edge of the palm. The shape of the fingertips could point them in the direction of building, carpentry, cook/chef/housekeeping, hairdressing, each showing the traits of the inner artisan. Physical labor and constructive work with the hands also appeals to them as spare-time occupations. Being practical thinkers, they could choose to become mechanical engineers.

These down to earth people have a love of home and the duties of home, yet they tend to restrict any form of demonstration of affection. The male of this type makes a good husband to a woman who does not expect or demand much passion, love, or warmth to be outwardly expressed. Unless the Mount of Venus is well developed he is likely to take things for granted forgetting to show little acts of affection.

The female with the practical square hand (and there are many more square-handed males than females) can be more demonstrative with her affections. If the Mount of Venus, which lies just below the thumb, is high and firm on either male or female or on both their hands, they are likely to be highly sexed, enjoy each other and love, marriage, home, and children will be important. The dour nature of the square hand will be filled with vitality and expression.

Hand Number 5 – Psychic

Number 5 is the Pointed – Psychic Hand belonging to the idealistic somewhat impractical person who finds it difficult to deal with the ups and downs of everyday life and its problems. The hand is generally long, thin and narrow, delicate and graceful with pointed fingers and almond shaped fingernails.

These people have precious little idea of order, they are rather undisciplined and infuriating along with their lack of punctuality. They are easily influenced by others and tend to confide in and trust anyone who is kind to them. Dreamy, intuitive and deeply sensitive, they have a great compassion and empathy for others and a longing to be surrounded by peace and harmony. This is all very fine, but it tends to lead to an unproductive life. Luckily, this true type of hand is very rare as the lines in the hand and the shape of finger tips will give more backbone to the vivid and creative imagination. This marvellous imagination produces excellent writers, poets, musicians, and composers, fantastic artists as color greatly appeals to them. In fact, some of these people have the ability to think, see, feel, and perhaps hear color in every tone of music, every joy and sorrow because every emotion for them is reflected in color. This ability is called Synesthesia and I talked about in my book *Seeds of the Soul*. We are all endowed with it, but a great percentage of people are totally unaware that it lies within them. It is a most valuable commodity to have if you are very artistic or extremely psychic.

Take a look at the Head line on the palm, (see Figure 1) and if it curves down towards the Mount of Luna, this will indicate a strong imagination. You will also find that you or the person whose palm you are looking at is in close contact with the deeper, subconscious side of life that tends to give the impression of being "dreamy." If there is any interest in religious thoughts and philosophies and the artistic side is extremely predominant, then religious paintings with that wonderful "dreamy" look could be executed and sold providing a very useful, constructive, productive life, bringing in a great deal of money. To bring out and develop these characteristics, this person will need to be dominated and more or less controlled by a stronger more active person who is able to understand and accept their passive, unstable emotional existence. Note that the person with this type of hand is frequently given to wallowing in sullen moods, thereby draining themselves of energy.

People with this type of hand are introverted, secretive, sealed up inside, and protective of self, giving the impression of being "cold," but in actual fact they are warm, and sympathetic deep down, not demonstrative, just rather sensitive and impressionable which leaves them confused about the conditions surrounding them. They seek to escape from the outside world and life in general and the lines and mounts on the hand will determine their particular strengths and weaknesses and whether their lives will amount to anything really constructive and artistic.

Talking about weaknesses, this type of hand is often without sufficient physical strength and this can be determined by looking carefully at the palm to see if there is a "Girdle of Venus." This particular feature deepens the desire to escape and live in a world of fantasy. Now, the Girdle, if there is one, will be found just above the heart line and you will see a half circle under the Mount of Saturn (the mount is under the middle Saturn finger) to the Mount of the Sun (the ring finger, often called the Apollo finger). It can form a complete or a fragmented ring beneath these fingers or there may be horizontal broken lines crossing the mounts. When the Girdle is extremely broken and fragmented with many broken lines across the top of the palm (below the Saturn and Sun fingers) this could well be an indication of ill health and nervous depression perhaps caused by an unhappy or discontented life. In this case it might be wise to suggest help/counseling to overcome the highly sensitive emotions before alcohol or drugs become the attraction.

To see what physical energy is available, look at the Saturn and Sun (Apollo) lines in the palm. They run from the wrist up through the palm to the bottom of each finger. If these lines hit the Girdle of Venus, the Girdle becomes a barrier causing a blockage and obstacle to the use of the physical energies. The energy then overflows into the palm itself causing a much higher sensitivity and nervousness that finally depletes the energy resources of the owner of this hand. There will be times of energy and times of exhaustion where rest is needed until the energy patterns are restored.

It is quite likely that there is a great deal of psychic ability here and the owner of this hand may wish to be part of the community as a professional psychic. In this case, energy patterns will be "all over the place," at times resulting in exhaustion because there is no "pacing" of the energy. More than likely, the owner of this hand who is a true psychic will live in two worlds, in touch with the energy of his/her soul and aware of their own group relationship on "the other side." If you are the "guiding light" of this person, you will eventually come to understand the ethereal, imaginative side of their existence, recognize the fickle inconstancy and offer the strong bond of love that is needed to hold the two of you together.

Hand Number 6 – Knotty/Philosophical

Number 6 is the Knotty – Philosophical hand. This is the hand of the thoughtful analytical person in search of wisdom and knowledge. The palm is large, well developed, bony with long fingers and well-developed joints on either side of the phalanges.

For this to be a true knotty/philosophical hand, the knots on the fingers *must* be quite obvious otherwise they should be assessed as being smooth. Look carefully at each finger. Some could be smooth and others with varying degrees of "knot" lining up on either the first or second phalange or both. We will look first at the hand that has obvious knots on all fingers, then we will look at the smooth fingers as this will adjust the qualities and traits of this hand.

The hand that is really knotty indicates great staying power and the ability for painstaking research. There is an aptitude for mathematics, a great appreciation for the exact sciences, and here we find people such as scientists, historians, engineers, navigators, architects, agriculturists – all these jobs requiring a great deal of knowledge. Their careful logical thinking leads them in this direction. They are patient and systematic, slow to arrive at conclusions and when they have reached them they will apply their own ideas to the situations they have been considering.

Truth and facts are what interest them most and in their search they can get too caught up and preoccupied with details. They tend to be somewhat introverted, like to go their own way and they don't really care what other people think of them. Many are unorthodox and eccentric in their search for truth and spirituality. These are the people who become writers, advisors, and philosophers. Their patience usually brings success in mental things, money holding less interest for them, as their desire is for knowledge and philosophies. Being so analytical, there is less emotion in these people. They are guided by reason (their head) not by impulse (heart) yet they will impress you with their common sense and philosophical conclusions.

Now the first joint/knot by the first phalange at the top of the finger deals purely with mental order – the qualities of the mind. The second knot represents the material side. One who loves neatness, and order in all material things. If there are knots on both phalanges, you will find both mental and material order, a person who acts more slowly, analyzing everything, reasoning, investigating before making conclusions, then keeping everything in apple pie order.

If there is only a knot at the top of the finger and the second is smooth, there is a very intelligent mind combined with systematic thinking. There is a lack of balance here as they are quite thoughtless about what they wear. Neither their personal appearance or money hold much interest for them. Here we see mind too much over matter. If the knot is only on the second finger joint, there is a very careful, systematic approach to material affairs. They will also pay much attention to their personal appearance, always wishing to make a good impression.

Finger tips are very important with the knotty/philosophical hand. Square tips get carried away by their systematic common-sense approach to life. They make life difficult for others as they are frequently strict disciplinarians, hard taskmasters, and they get caught up in a lot of unnecessary red tape. The spatulate tip, although materially useful, can be a cranky person and extremely obstinate. These two types with knotty joints don't believe in anything they cannot see or touch. They are skeptical of everything until they have proof – their proof. The conic tip is ideal for the knotty hand. It lightens the character bringing a touch of idealism and an appreciation of beauty and art, and if the tips are a mix of square and conical there will be a great understanding of the metaphysical aspects of life and a sympathetic attitude towards the less fortunate of this world. This hand often belongs to world leaders.

As I mentioned earlier, not all fingers on the philosophical hand will be knotty. This will alter the characteristics here and there as smooth fingers usually indicate a certain amount of impulsiveness. In the case of the knotty hand this is a blessing, giving a lightness to the nit-picking overly strong analytical tendency.

Look carefully at the fingers and see which have obvious knots and those that are smooth. Is it the first (Jupiter) finger, the second (Saturn), the third (Sun) or the little Mercury finger. With Jupiter they are likely to pay more attention to their clothing, surroundings, the home and its decorations, and even their religion. Obviously they will pay more attention to earning/gaining money to be able to afford what they want. With the Saturn finger they will be more agreeable and pleasant companions rather than spending so much time alone.

The more smooth fingers the knotty hand has the greater the sense and appreciation of beauty. There is less reliance on reason and analysis, more fluency in thought and speech – it is easier for them to express themselves. If there are a number of smooth fingers, they could fall into the trap of allowing their inspirations and intuitions to lead them astray, causing them to make some hasty decisions at times. If there is a strong, deep Head line on the palm, this could well come to their rescue, stopping them from making errors at the last moment as reason steps in to control the haste. You can see now how adding all these nifty little bits and pieces alters the character analysis you've already found. The later two chapters on the lines of the palm will bring more interesting information that will really start bringing the character analysis to life.

Hand Number 7 – Mixed

Number 7 is the Mixed Hand. This hand is a thorough mix of the previous six shapes. It is the hand of versatility combining creativity with practicality, yet oftentimes it is applied in an erratic fashion. Adaptable to both people and circumstances, rarely reacting to the ups and downs of life, a type of "hail fellow, well met" sort of person. They love new ideas, restless in both body and mind, never staying long in one place, or carrying out to the finish the ideas they have. Dozens of projects get started, and as they fail, they become abandoned. Being rather unstable and likely to be a "Jack of all Trades," they rarely succeed completely in anything, a big starter and a little finisher or one who has big plans and not much action. But, the shape of the fingers and their tips will most definitely alter the basic reading, and with this hand you may again, find a mixture of all six. Look carefully and take note of how much of all the other hand types are incorporated here. Is the person clever, a good conversationalist, diplomatic, and tactful? Creative in the way of playing a musical instrument or painting, and drawing? Is there an ability for acting, singing, dancing, writing? Look directly at the palm as a strong Head line is required to successfully utilize any talents that are shown.

For instance, a pointed Jupiter finger (1st finger) indicates caution and intelligence in different situations. Optimistic and sociable, they are gifted conversationalists, likely showing up any leadership qualities. A conical finger tip says they are intellectual and talented idealists but emotions can get in the way. The square finger tip brings out business acumen and the spatulate are pragmatic. They enjoy travel and outdoor life.

On the Saturn finger (middle finger) this shows a good sense of responsibility, firming up any practicality shown in the hand and the dreamy, visionary qualities of the pointed fingers could be incorporated into a career.

With the conical tip on Saturn, those runaway emotions will be reined in quite nicely, Saturn is not emotional – too wise for that.

The Sun finger – the ring finger (often called the Apollo finger) is the most creative on the hand. The pointed finger is not seen here quite so much as the other shapes, but when it appears on the ring finger, there is a tendency to live in a world of fantasy. They are not particularly interested in the material and practical side of life and to make anything of their artistic gifts, they will need to have a very functional and disciplined nature. Through lack of focus and direction they can lose everything. Now the conical fingertip offers practical artistic creation in the areas of art, music, acting, or even behind the scenes as a director, editor, or an agent to artists. The square fingertip is also not often seen, but when it shows up you will find practical creativity in the line of architecture, engineering. Combined with a very square hand it can indicate the creative artist who can become famous due to bringing logic into the world of fantasy. The spatulate tip points to the inventors, explorers and the pioneers of new ways of large-scale manufacturing and the organization of industries.

The little finger of Mercury is the communicator. With a pointed tip, there may be quite a bit of psychism, possibly as a spiritual advisor, as they seem to be well connected to the spiritual realm. Certainly they can draw on their imagination and indulge in flights of fantasy. They can also be astute and rather sarcastic, especially if they take a dislike to the aura of another person. The conic tip brings out creativity and an artistic streak. Quick and witty, they enjoy people, they make excellent salespersons and their eloquence wins people over. These are the people often involved in TV talk shows, particularly if they have square tips where they talk on practical subjects. They have good business sense translating theory into practice so their ventures usually make money. The spatulate tip indicates a magnetic speaker whose words can move the masses. Here is an original thinker with practical ability.

If you look back on the earlier chapter on hand types, you will find the finger tips show up much of what is indicated in the hand shapes. As you learn more and more about palmistry you will see how the palms, thumbs, fingers, tips, and the mounts reflect each other, firming up the character you are building. We will talk more about the fingers a little later on, right now we will get into the mounts under the fingers in the next chapter and both sides of the character, positive and negative, will really come to light. The mounts will also confirm the type of person you are. Do you come under the influence of Jupiter, Saturn, Sun, Mercury, Mars, Venus, Moon? Let's find out.

Mounts Under the Fingers

Chapter 4

Figure 4:
Laws of Scientific Hand Reading
W. Benham

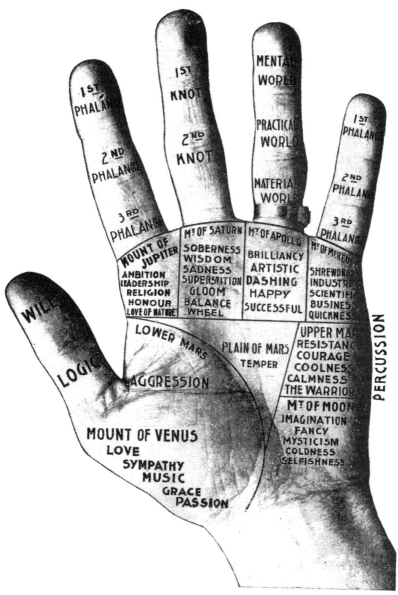

Benham, W. The Laws of Scientific Hand Reading.
Duell, Sloan and Pierce, NY, NY, 1900, 1946, 1966

Hold out your hand now, look under the base of the fingers and you will see some raised little humps there. Some are quite plump and raised, others are flat, some fingers have none at all. Each of these are called mounts and they are the keys to our natural abilities and emotional traits. Lines and other markings on the hand – these come up in Chapter Six – show how these traits are used.

Just as we had seven types of hands that we've previously investigated, so we have seven mounts on the hand to define those qualities you will add to or subtract from the character you have already developed and written up in your notebook. Besides the four mounts under the fingers you will find the other three actually on the palm: two at the side of the hand – the Mount of the Moon and the Upper Mars – and the other at the base of the thumb called the Mount of Venus that I mentioned in Chapter Two.

I have included here a diagram of the mounts from William Benham's most excellent book *The Laws of Scientific Hand Reading* which is a *must* for anyone who is or wishing to be a professional palmist. His diagram gives working keywords of the traits/qualities attached to each mount. These are the distinguishing features of the character or the quality of mind you have discerned from the previous chapters, either adding strength or pointing to a weakness that may have been missed.

Look carefully at each of these mounts, note which is the strongest. The prominent ones are the strongest, flat mounts don't have much to say, but occasionally you will see deep depressions or what look like small holes where the mounts should be. These indicate a weakness or a lack of the qualities of that particular mount. Sometimes you will find a mount is pulled to one side by the greater strength of another giving a reading of the mix of both mounts.

If there are two equally developed mounts then you will have a combination of two types. For instance, the Jupiter mount (under the first finger) and the Mercury mount (little finger) are both well developed, then Mercury will impose either scientific or oratorical qualities onto the Jupiter character elevating his/her ambition.

Each mount has a strong and a weak side like the types of hands. Each finger and each mount have the same name just as the finger tips have the same names as the types/shapes of hands. They all interact with each other giving strength to the character and showing up the weaknesses that can be altered and strengthened if recognized and worked on.

Jupiter

Starting off with Jupiter, the first finger that everyone points with, does it have a mount beneath it? Is it well developed, raised and puffy?

Jupiter's qualities here are the same as those in an astrology chart namely ambition, pride, a desire for power and if the mount is well developed it points to leadership and a desire for command. Politicians, devout religious leaders, university professors, academics in high positions, mayors of communities, bank owners and managers, high court justices, and those who deal at a high level with law, and legal affairs, science and medicine all come under the influence of Jupiter. With a good mount they earn respect and a good reputation through their efficiency and the power to influence and shape matters.

Jupiter represents luck and fortune. The expansive, optimistic energy of the owner of this mount attracts opportunity, prosperity, with which to get the good things in life, and these seemingly flow abundantly with very little effort. Marriage at an early age is happy and there is generally an excellent relationship with their children (possibly over indulgence) who also are likely to have fortunate lives.

This well-favored mount indicates tremendous independence, one who is frank, open, and having a philosophic attitude towards life. When friends and relatives run into difficult situations, this paragon of virtue will be there with help and compassion.

What I have expressed here represents the so called "true" Jupiterian type, something we will never find as there are always modifications to be made as we have seen in previous chapters. In fact, what you have already learned about finger lengths, tips and the three phalanges you will apply to the readings of all the mounts as these will alter the basic indication of the mount.

Looking further at this mount, the strong Jupiterian is of medium height with a big strong build, large lungs from which emanates a rich musical voice both speaking and singing. The voice is frequently loud, full of confidence and self assertion. In fact, as they are quite aware they own these qualities, it tends to make them somewhat vain. They like to hear the sound of their own voice and to see the results of the impressions they make on others, shaping their views and actions. A little weakness here, hardly recognized by their followers as they are frequently given kind words of comfort when needed along with money or other necessities, especially towards the Church as they are often deeply religious. Recall Chapter Three and what I said about inherited religious influences from the parents? This Jupiter mount will show up the influence and which way it will be applied: with great zeal pomp and show, a heavy hand

and domineering manner, or even an agnostic leaning following no creed or Church. If Jupiter's finger tip is spatulate, this agnostic leaning is quite likely – take a good look at it.

If the hand itself is of a spatulate type, this individual will have a knack for organizing others and if the mount is high – situated right under the base of the finger, you will find a lively individualistic character with a great deal of personal magnetism and business acumen. But that high mount, especially if it is soft and broad, shows a tendency towards waste and self indulgence. The main weakness here is over enjoyment of life, high living, a fondness for highly seasoned food, love of wine, all adding excess flesh and weight to an already large body. This all adds up to health problems such as gout, stomach and lung troubles, indigestion, stroke/paralysis and others, all of which could be avoided. Another point with this spatulate finger tip, they like the outdoor life – along with travel – so exercise and activity could help to keep the weight down. There will be a more practical outlook on life and they might even be able to spot their own weaknesses especially where their health is concerned.

Continuing on with the finger tips, if it is a square tip business acumen and practicality will be added to their ambition – remember this is the finger of power, ambition and status. Square hand, and square tips are very useful types to have along with a square mark on the mount of Jupiter and this square gives protection to all endeavors ensuring success. The pointed tip will add caution and intelligence and the conical tip shows an intellectual and talented idealist who is likely to let emotions get in the way of accomplishments yet the square mark will still give a certain amount of protection against failure.

We talked about finger lengths in a previous chapter and you must apply that information here as well. Is the Jupiter finger a normal length – about $4/5^{ths}$ in length of the second finger? There is plenty of initiative here and a moderate amount of ambition combined with enough tenaciousness without being too pushy.

If the finger is long – almost the same length as the second finger, this shows domineering leadership qualities with a love of power and a tendency towards arrogance and intolerance. An extremely long finger is indicative of a cruel and dictatorial nature that could have been handed down from the male side of the family. Take a good look at the type/shape of hand. A short finger shows a strong dislike of responsibility and a lack of confidence that stems from the early life. Take a look at the right hand and compare it with the left to see if any positive changes have taken place

boosting the self confidence. Remember the left hand is the passive one – what you are born with and the right one shows what you have done with your talents and abilities.

Recall the phalanges on the thumb we talked about in Chapter Two? Each one of the fingers also has a set. The top phalange, closest to the finger tip is the mental world. The middle one points to the material things of life and the bottom one, close to the mounts deals with the sensual side of the nature. Depending on the length of each of these phalanges you will be able to see the type of influence they have on what you have discovered so far. If all three are about the same length, then they carry a very nice balance of the person's views and interaction with the world in which he/she lives. If the top one is the longest, intellectual and mental matters will serve to control over-weaning pride and help to alter other excesses that show up in the reading. Intuition may well be brought to the forefront of the mind, along with religious thoughts and contemplation of the mysteries of life. The middle phalange points to applying ambitions to the business world. If the third one is the longest, then gluttony will likely be the downfall causing the ill health I mentioned previously.

Back to the mounts again. If any mount is not directly under the finger but pulled to one side, it will take on some of the qualities of the mount to which it is leaning. With the Jupiter mount leaning towards the Saturn finger this will temper the over exuberance, over eating, extravagance of any kind. There is not quite so much joy in life and confidence in self which is really a good thing as all achievements will be more worthwhile because they will be of a conservative and more solid nature. There will be more intellectual leanings and scholastic attainments especially if the actual finger also leans towards Saturn. But if the mount is both high and over large conceit over mental accomplishments will need to be controlled.

If the mount leans towards the outer side of the palm, pride in family takes precedence. It may be the heritage – descended from important people; pride in parents/in laws and their social prestige. His/her children will be expected and encouraged to attain certain distinction in life and this could well be the main ambition.

Now, a flat mount indicates a dull personality and one who has little confidence and almost certainly lacking in self respect – a very poor Jupiterian specimen. On the other hand, an over developed mount produces an egotistical, arrogant, proud individual. With this particular type you may see a great deal of charm, attentiveness, and what seems to be consideration and interest in others.

This is only on the surface. Underneath could lie a cold, calculating nature set on revenge if opposed or considered to be outwitted. Check out the fingers. If they are straight up and close set you will find a large streak of meanness with a stiff intolerant nature.

Further indication of this weakness is if the lower Mars mount is very large and it and the Jupiter mount join the line of Head. You will find further confirmation if there are grilles or horizontal lines on the lower Mars mount. To view these I suggest you buy a six inch magnifying glass, you will need it later on when we look at the lines and marks on the hand.

Note also the color of the skin. If there is even a tinge of yellow, the blood is likely to be poisoned through over eating and drinking (possibly an alcoholic) and this will encourage any vicious tendencies. Any sign of redness in the skin – not pink but a real red – points to anger that may well be hidden deep within this revengeful person. Remember that long fingers are fond of detail and minutiae so if revenge is apparent in this individual, a campaign against a foe will be planned with utmost care and will very likely succeed without the recipient knowing where it came from.

We've covered a multitude of things here and there are many more interesting matters that I will cover bit by bit through each mount. With this Jupiter mount we talked about health, the virtues and vices of Jupiter, touched on skin color, added what was learned about the type of hand, the thumb, and its three phalanges.

You have noted the type of qualities from the finger phalanges – mental strength, business interests and acumen, or more inclined to the sensual and material aspects of life; and the finger tips – practical, active, artistic, or an ideas person. You looked at the fingers – reason and analysis if knotty ruled or inspiration was the guiding factor with smooth fingers. Long and short – detailed or quickness of mind.

Pull all this together in your notebook, adding and subtracting from what you have deduced and finally, take a closer look at the thumb phalanges. Does the top phalange show enough will power and determination to bring these qualities to fruition? Can the second phalange be applied at the same time for balance? Now you can decide if this person shows enough influences to indicate a Jupiter character. If not, move onto further mounts, study again covering all the same angles that we've previously been through and eventually you will arrive at a complete character analysis. The character you have discovered represents the destiny shown by the left hand and in Chapter Six you will be able to see how the principle lines on the right hand

have shaped and altered the destiny by applying these qualities and traits. Now onto the mount of Saturn.

Before we actually start in on this second mount, I would like to mention that what you have learned in the previous three chapters, you will first apply to every hand reading. These are the basics that you start with each time – the hand type/shape, then the thumb and all it contains in that chapter, along with the knowledge of the phalanges, fingers, and tips. It sounds like a lot but when you have been doing this for quite a while much will be committed to memory and you will find yourself automatically making your mental notes.

Saturn

When you start looking at the mounts, here's where you will see the differences in each one. What you will discover in this Saturn mount is totally different to the Jupiter mount, although each mount can enhance the other. For instance, if the Jupiter mount or finger is leaning towards Saturn, where Jupiter's over-exuberance needed to be reined in and controlled, this same joy of life would be of great benefit to Saturn who tends to be a somewhat cynical sober-sides, often taking a gloomy and cautious approach to life.

Luckily, this mount of Saturn that is underneath the second finger is rarely highly developed. In fact you will find either Jupiter's mount or Apollo's mount, or even both, leaning towards the place where Saturn's mount should be. You will find a dip or hollow there instead with some sort of marking on it. That's good for the Saturn finger/mount as this will give the qualities of Jupiter or Apollo to Saturn, removing its "wet-blanket" repressive effect. That flat mount also turns this Saturnian into an optimistic, outgoing person.

Saturn stands for structure, rules, regulations and control. Without these in our daily lives we would be dealing with mayhem most of the time. Can you imagine what it would be like without organized traffic control? It's bad enough when we come to those four way stops and nobody knows whose turn it is next – especially at rush hour when everyone is going to or coming home from work. Just think about having no traffic lights at all, an unorganized transit system, no organized system within the schools, or the planet itself with no organized government control. This is just one area of Saturn's positive side in our daily existence.

The good points that you will note in the hand you are reading are its excellent organizing and executive ability. There is a responsible, patient, intellectual approach to life, and a stability in the way duty and work are handled. Saturn tends to be restrictive, but it works in a positive fashion

and also a negative way depending on what marks or lines are on the mount or where the mount should be. A single vertical line here will increase the strength of the Saturn approach to life producing a rather profound, deep individual. In terms of the revered university professor these traits are excellent. In the average person with an ordinary every day job these can be a deterrent, the character comes across as being rather formidable. Because Saturn itself is structured, its influence in the lives of the strong Saturnian tends to have them compute, analyze and reason out every area of life – they insist on knowing every detail from beginning to end, taking their time in decision making. This also applies to the emotional areas of their lives leaving them somewhat unloved until the right person – if ever – comes along. This individual most definitely needs enthusiasm and warmth and we may well find it when we look at the other mounts that may affect the Saturn finger and also the phalanges on the finger itself. Let's just finish the portrait of the "true" Saturnian before looking at the adjusting factors.

The Saturnian is usually the tallest of the seven types. In total contradiction to the shape of the Jupiterian type, these Saturn types are often thin – gaunt in some species; even the women, with a sallow, perhaps yellowish skin that is frequently rough and dry. The hair is black, straight, thick, and coarse, cheekbones are high on a long face and the eyebrows are thick growing together over the nose and turning up at the ends. A most distinctive type. In fact, if you take a look at a photograph of Abraham Lincoln this will give you an idea of what to look for. He is a perfect specimen of a Saturn type.

Saturn is a difficult area to write about in a positive constructive manner. An over abundance of its "good" points – being too well organized, over responsible, and very economical – can become faults. Living totally by rules and being so buttoned up keeps the rest of the world at bay, hence a somewhat lonely person who may not have the opportunity to achieve his/her potential.

The Saturnian type unwittingly sets boundaries, rules and limitations, this being its natural characteristic, which is all very fine when it comes to governments, hierarchies, the ruling of the people, and the world in general. When it comes down to the single individual, then the qualities of its nature need the *joi de vivre* of Jupiter, the versatility and appreciation of beauty and the arts from Apollo, and the cheerfulness and humor of Mercury. These are essential for the balance of Saturn.

Saturn has a natural love of solitude, its sober sides prefers a good book rather than people and is not too interested in having friends. Perhaps just one good reliable person with whom to spend an occasional evening discussing the deeper aspects of life is often enough for this somewhat anti-social person. If these strong indications show up in the finger/mount this person is likely to choose occupations where contact with people is kept to a minimum. Preferring country life to the noise of the city, agriculture, farm life, laboratory work, horticulture, botany, and floristry have great appeal.

Another area of great intrigue for them is the exploration of oil, coal, and minerals in which they are frequently successful. These Saturn people are fascinated by the occult and mysteries. Those who have writing ability, and many do, are often successful in writing ghost stories, histories, mystery novels, and scientific books and articles.

Look carefully at the mount, even though it is not evident, see if there is a triangle, a circle, a trident, a single vertical line or a square on this space. There may even be a combination here. Note that this will increase the strength of this mount showing more than ordinary development and if the mounts on the other fingers bring help and lightness to these characteristics, you will find a very interesting person. If you find a cross, a grille, an island or a crossbar on the mount, these will indicate defects of the character producing a morbid, melancholy, gloomy, rather pessimistic and stingy person. The stronger the Saturn indications the more avaricious the person is likely to be. There will also be health problems such as rheumatism, varicose veins, hemorrhoids, and quite likely liver problems, internal disorders and an excess of bile. This latter will be indicated by a very thick lower phalange on the finger and a bend at the top phalange leaning towards the finger of Apollo. If you see spots or small islands on the Head line, just under the mount of Saturn, teeth and ear troubles will probably show up sometime during the life. Study the Figure 9 in Chapter 9 of "marks to look for."

To see how much Saturn development there is (and hopefully not too much), you must look at the fingers and mounts for the balance, including the mounts situated on the palm of the hand which you will learn about in the next chapter.

As we already know – long fingers are a sign of patience and a love of detail, and on Saturn, it points to the intellectual person. If the finger is extra long, here is the bore – the pedant – whose intellectual dryness tends to drive people away. Short fingers show impatience and a reliance more on intuition, along with quick thought and action, something that Saturn could use. What length is that Saturn finger?

Now look at the phalanges. If the first is longest, this person will be occupied by the mental world. Here is the thinker, always the student wanting to know more. It backs up the superstitious nature and the inclination to delve into and write about the occult sciences. If the second phalange is the longest, this points to the business side of Saturn including scientific investigations, chemistry, history, and mathematics, plus farming, horticulture, and agriculture. The third phalange indicates a love of money. You will have to decide from what you have previously discovered whether the person is economical or just plain greedy and miserly.

You already know what the fingertip shapes stand for. Look at Saturn's tip – is it square, spatulate, conical, pointed? Whatever it is, add that to your notes. Finally, we shall see how the other mounts and fingers are influencing the Saturn qualities and traits and more of the picture will come to life until it is altered once again by the lines and marks in the following chapters.

First of all, if the base of the fingers are in a straight line this often indicates an ambitious personality. If there is a gentle curve here from one side to the other, this person is likely to be quite balanced with a strong inspirational link between the soul and the mind. But if the line moves from one side and curves up to the other making a "v" shape, take note, there is a great deal of insecurity here.

If the Apollo (third) finger is leaning towards the Saturn finger this will add a great deal of brightness, joy, happiness, and laughter to the dull, dreary personality, awakening an appreciation of beauty, perhaps even the ability to become an artist or musician. This leaning finger gives grace and tact to Saturn and if the Jupiter finger also leans towards Saturn, the deep emotions, usually kept hidden will be stirred within this cool character. Jupiter's strong leaning will encourage Saturn to consider the law as an occupation. Saturn has great respect for justice and Jupiter likes to give orders – both Saturn and Jupiter like to be obeyed. One other thing you should note: if Jupiter and Saturn both lean towards each other this indicates an emotionally insecure person, yet one who is assertive in business matters.

Remember to look closely at the thumb for its size and note how much willpower there is to accomplish the choice of lifestyle and if there is enough logic from the second phalange to be applied for the essential balanced state of mind. This is most necessary for Saturn, for if there is an imbalance of the anima/animus, this will affect the self-expression of the individual, especially where emotions and the love nature is concerned. At the best of times, Saturn is not particularly amorous – the opposite sex not being too impressed with the quiet nature, but the Apollo finger, and the Venus and Mars mounts may well alter this attitude. Let's take a look at the Apollo mount and finger and see what more it has to offer to Saturn in the way of helping it to warm up and open up.

Saturn in its turn offers something to each one of the mounts by restraining their over exuberance, enthusiasm and passion. Saturn indeed, is the counter-acting influence in the hand.

Apollo

The Apollo finger is often called the Sun finger or the ring finger, and the finger itself points to growth, luck, fame, and fortune – all things being equal! Where is the mount situated? Is it right under the finger or pulled to one side towards the Mercury finger or the Saturn finger? Is it high up under the finger or sitting close to the Heart line? If the mount tends to lean towards the Saturn area, this will give seriousness towards any accomplishment, and there will be an appreciation of Saturn's help in making plans. This is one of the benefits from Saturn. If the Sun mount leans towards the Mercury side a practical business mind is added to the Sun's talents – which are many – plus a certain amount of shrewdness in all business dealings. Saturn's other benefit here is that it gives the Sun the understanding that they both have a need to satisfy (to balance) family and business commitments equally in order to feel content – each can give to the other what is necessary. The Sun informs Saturn that in order to stay healthy, happy, and vigorous, it is necessary to take time out for play and laughter which is so necessary to liven up the brain that Saturn frequently overworks by its studious nature and desire for being alone. With Jupiter being occupied with exalting itself a lot of the time and Saturn being absorbed in its seriousness, the Sun with its light and brightness points out the beauty of life.

This mount and finger is frequently designated as being a total creative artist, a painter, writer, musician, song writer, dancer or whatever, but this is not so. There are actually two types of Sun people, both creative in their different ways.

To actually be the true creative artist, not just one who is a lover of art and beauty, to start with, the mount should be nicely developed with a little bump right in the center. There should be a long finger, a long first phalange and a fine, deep Line of Apollo running up the center of the palm, all these pointing to fame depending on what is done with the production of the creative talents and how and where they are applied. If there are stars on the mount – even better – these promise quite a fortune.

There is a lot of difference between the two Sun types. Granted they both have creative talent, but this second type applies it to the business world where again, a lot of money is waiting to be made. The love of art and beauty is naturally ingrained in both types, but the business type does not have the actual creative artistic power to produce works of art. The creative urges and feelings here lead to intuitively understanding what the public needs and what it will buy. All choices are done with a tasteful eye, and such natural grace, versatility, and charm automatically draws people towards him/her. The indications to look for here are a high mount right up under the Apollo finger and there are quite likely to be several vertical lines on the mount pointing to a multiplicity of talents.

All Sun people have many skills and if those vertical lines on the mount are crossed by one or more lines – this is a weakness. There are too many talents here causing a diversion of interest and unless recognized and corrected it will lead to a Jack of all Trades, nothing much coming to fruition except frustration and a lousy reputation for being unreliable.

This Sun type who also appreciates art and beauty is successful in business rather than being the real creative artist. Nevertheless, the creative eye is used in arranging business surroundings which impresses clients, chooses goods for sale with unerring judgment – clothing, jewels, artwork, anything of beauty that will appeal to the public, making money easily. This second type is highly intuitive, more so than the previous type, from which he/she can quickly grasp an idea making something new from something old, frequently making a fortune. They also seem to be able to make money on the stock market and the gaming tables, but if there is a cross on the mount with no Line of Apollo there will likely be poor judgment in speculation. If there is an over-developed mount, there will be a tendency to over-rate abilities, and a grille on the mount suggests an exaggerated idea of the talents; but on the other hand, if the line of Sun reaches into the cross along with horizontal lines, there will be many obstacles to overcome. Eventually, success in business will be reached, but it will take lot of hard work.

Usually, the Sun person is healthy, happy, and vigorous, but everybody has weak health points. Sun people frequently have weak eyes and are also prone to a heart condition. To check up on the eyes, look for a small dot or island on the Head line under the mount. The give away for a heart problem is an island or dot on the Heart line and a tendency for the finger nails to have a blue sheen.

Before you finish assessing the Sun person, apply the finger and phalange lengths. If the Sun and Jupiter finger are the same lengths, there will be a beautiful balance of ambition and brilliance. If the Sun finger is longer than the Saturn finger there will be strong gambling tendencies and a foolhardy nature.

With the first phalange being the longest, the artist, the writer, the poet, in fact all artistic tendencies, will come to the fore. If the second phalange is the longest – here is the clever business person. Now, if these two phalanges are equal in length, the artistic talent and the business world will be combined and if there is a circle on the mount as well, fame will come to this person.

Not so for the third phalange if it is the longest. This points to the show off, the flashy person who has a desire for money but not much talent, and no taste for the artistic and beautiful things in life. Any redeeming qualities for this phalange will be seen from the lines and marks on the hands.

Your final touch for this cheerful, charming person is reading the finger tips, judging the thumb indications, then putting it altogether.

Mercury

Now we come to the last finger on the hand before moving into the mounts on the palm. This is the little finger known as the Mercury finger. It's mount is found under the finger, but once again it can be pulled to one side towards the Sun mount or to the other side called the percussion – the outer side of the palm.

The Mercurian types are the most interesting of the four fingers and mounts as they are a mixture of so many different elements. The "good" Mercurian is one of the most successful of all the types being very shrewd, an excellent judge of human nature, and extremely intuitive. The other side of the Mercurian character produces the greatest liars, thieves, and swindlers applying the same abilities to their chosen profession as mentioned above. Their skillful hands makes them excellent pick pockets!

They are eloquent public speakers with a wonderful sense of humor – more than likely to have been the one chosen in high school or college to make a speech. They excel in the law profession due to their shrewdness and their way with words. They are also very successful in medicine and they are in their element in business, scientific areas, or as writers. How do you know if your subject is a Mercurian? Look at the mount under the little finger. If it is right under the finger, well developed and the little finger is long and large, the person is of compact build, not too tall and has a very expressive face – here is your Mercurian.

If there are numerous small vertical lines on the mount along with a long second phalange and finger, the major interest here will be for the medical profession. Prominent and successful doctors are likely to have these

markings, dedicated nurses will also have some or all of them. It is called the "Medical Stigmata."

The Mercurian, being a restless type, is fond of travel. If money permits, they will take all available opportunities to visit countries around the world. Variety is the spice of life to them. These travel lines are shown by many lines on the palm starting from the Mount of the Moon, (on the outside of the palm) running up to the Mercury mount. If there isn't sufficient money for this indulgence, the next best choice will be to either own or work for a travel agency where the perks of reduced or free travel are available. If there is a slight inward curve of the finger, ownership of the agency is more than likely and it will make money through the shrewd business brain. A triangle on the Mercury mount will show success in business. A star on the mount augers well if the choice of profession is in a scientific area or if the person becomes an inventor. A puffy mount points an intellectual side.

If the mount leans towards the Sun finger, there will be a practical interest in the arts and antique fields as a career. If the Head line points up towards this leaning mount this person will also be a collector of art and antiques.

The mount leaning towards upper Mars (see Figure 4) shows an indomitable spirit – one who will fight for a cause and we have many people today who are under this influence.

With no mount showing on the hand, there is a lack of business ability and not much aim in life.

If the mount is over developed this is indicative of a high pressure salesman also one of an inventive mind. This works in two ways. If the finger is quite crooked, this person is likely to be of the baser type of Mercury – a "con" person who uses an inventive mind to find an easy life and easy money, and makes his/her way through life cheating the rest of humanity.

This leads me into the psychic realm where easy pickings are available for these clever Mercurians from the inordinate amount of people who desire readings. These "readers" do not need to know a great deal of palmistry, they use the knowledge gained from the size and shape of the thumb – as I mentioned in Chapter Two. This is the great giveaway of the person's character and they use this and their natural shrewdness along with their well-developed intuition. This information is usually enough for the charlatan to capture the client's attention and amazement. Many people who go in for psychic readings are like an open book, their faces are full of expressions, so it is easy for the charlatan to give an "impressive" reading. Because the clients are so impressed, they do not realize that the reader asks questions of them. They unwittingly give the

reader this information which is then handed back to them in a different shape impressing the client even more. Clever isn't it? Didn't I say the Mercurian has an inventive mind? Look for a cross on the mount of Mercury; this should set off bells for you indicating a "double dealing" person.

I haven't made any reference to health problems here as Mercury really only suffers from nervousness due to its high energy content keeping the person "on the go." The result of over-high nervous activity is dyspepsia – painful indigestion – that goes away when the nerves are calmed. Any other problems will show up on the Health and Life lines coming up in a later chapter.

Having made an assessment of all this information you have gathered, now you must apply the shape of the finger tips, phalanges, and the thumb, then make your adjustments to the personality you have defined.

We will move on now to the mounts on the palm of the hand that will give you further insight into either yourself or your client.

Mounts
on
the
Palm

Chapter 5

Figure 5:
Mounts in Palm

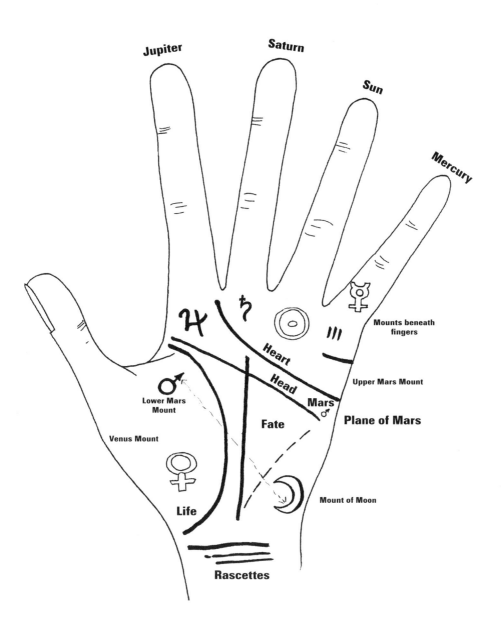

I mentioned earlier, the mounts are the keys to our natural abilities and emotional traits. You learned from the beginning of the book that the thumb and the shape of the hands are the keys to your character. The fingers, and particularly the mounts beneath them, add definition to the type of character, i.e., a Jupiterian type or a Saturnian, a Sun type or a Mercurian.

The mounts on the palm indicate the emotions, and combining these with the finger mounts shows how the emotional response sets the personality in motion. I mentioned in the previous chapter how the Mercury mount and the upper Mars mount coming together would spark the Martian response to fight for a cause – the resistance fighter. Now, if the Sun mount had been activated by upper Mars, the response would be lively and colorful paintings from the artist or bright, colorful martial music from the composer. To Jupiter's mount, it would encourage opportunism for leadership and the Saturn mount would hold back Mars impetuosity – the action without thought of the consequences – and resolve issues in a more circumspect way. The other palm mounts, the Moon (imagination and mysticism) Venus (love and passion) and the aggression of Lower Mars would bring other influences to bear on the finger mounts showing the different emotional responses to life events.

Mount of the Moon

Look on the outside of the palm (called the percussion side) opposite the thumb, just below the Upper Mars mount, this area is called the Mount of the Moon. As usual, there are two sides to this energy pattern. One is the wonderful power of imagination – the ability to form mental pictures. It would seem that the greater the vocabulary, the more ideas will be produced, and when the mount of Mercury is also involved, they will be expressed in many ways including new scientific findings. Musicians, composers, fiction and romance writers, perhaps history writers, if the Saturn mount is involved. People who speak many languages are influenced by the Moon and Mercury mounts and with the combination of the Sun mount, we see the emergence of poets, painters, and metaphysicians. The other side of this Moon energy is the lazy, selfish, over imaginative, restless, discontented, superstitious trouble-maker. The attitude of this person is a right pain! A good thing we don't have too many of these as other mounts, lines, and marks make alterations to the character.

The shape and size of this Moon mount is important. It can bulge in some places or bulge all over. It can be thin and nearly flat. It can have a lot of lines or few and it can be colorful or pale, all these things having different meanings. If the mount has a decided outward bulge it is called well developed; if it is also thick and forms a large pad on the inside of the hand then it is an extremely strong mount. If that bulge and thickness is very large and leans on the outside of the palm, here is an extreme Moon person who needs to be guided towards physical activity combined with some creative project, otherwise any talent will be simply fanciful and foolish leading nowhere.

There are people who have this bulge and thickness on the outside of the palm who think they have no talent because they have never been directed in childhood to express their ambitions, and they finally end up becoming the lazy Moon type, physically, mentally, dreaming dreams, frequently melancholy, superstitious, and hiding behind over-blown mysticism.

Take a look at the length of the first (Jupiter) finger and if it is shorter than the third finger, it indicates an inferiority complex stemming from dire poverty, the person not having the backbone to rise above the circumstances thereby retreating into him/herself. On the other hand, the child could have been "put down" by being compared to other people and being told "useless" or "no good" or "won't amount to anything," etc. As the child grew, a greater and greater uncertainty of self took place, feelings of not being able to cope satisfactorily with developing circumstances. Eventually, as the child became adult, it retreated into laziness along with a total dissatisfaction of life that will be shown by the Apollo line that leads up to the base of the third finger. Stultification, brought on by self preservation, then the lack of development of the intelligence and creativity is finally covered over by the sense of fear, the rationalization being: Don't disturb the physical or the emotional or you'll end up with discomfort of some sort.

Psychologically, self preservation and comfort are at the top of the list for everybody, even if it is unrecognized, somehow or another they will achieve it in either a positive or negative fashion. With this latter viewpoint, as the sensitive Moon person watches self being destroyed by the power of the inferiority complex, the anxiety increases over self preservation. It is not really surprising that some over-developed Lunar types with confused or fanciful thinking hide behind a variety of mysticism. Underneath all that fear and self preservation, this person with the inferiority complex could possibly be a genius. What is

required is the uncovering of the talents that are shown in the shape/type of hand, the strength of purpose in the thumb, and the directive control of the Saturn finger. Then look at the line of Apollo for success, and also see what fate – the Line of Destiny has in store. When it comes to handling one's own individual destiny, it literally is in our own hands. The events are written there to see and develop, to make something of ourselves, and it is the emotional reaction to the events that count.

The type of hand that really benefits from this Moon mount is the practical, productive square hand. The large and heavy mount on this hand, and it is usually the only hand that has it, is the basic force in bringing a strong creative potential into external manifestation. Because the attributes of the Moon are in the subconscious (hidden from the light) and in passive form, it requires and must be given external direction. Without it, there is just day-dreaming and nothing much done with the creative imagination as I mentioned earlier. This square hand with the Moon and mount, especially if it is developed towards Upper Mars is the practical dreamer who will apply imaginative ideas to the needs of every day. Physical activity will also be involved, and relaxation would take shape in the form of boxing, martial arts, football, building or carpentry, all of which have a rhythm this practical type appreciates.

Check on the finger tips, these will give more information on this Moon person. If they are pointed, this subject is likely to be most impractical, caught up in religious fervor and great idealism – always yearning for the impossible and unattainable.

Conic tips add intuitive qualities along with fanciful and romantic ideas. Belonging to the lazy class they need a boost to get them to use their creativity. Square tips we know are the practical ones.

Spatulate tips add activity to this already restless Moon person, particularly if the mount has a grille or is cross-lined. Nevertheless, their ideas are original, and unconventional but they may be too flighty to put them to good use. If they are lucky enough to have a smooth Lunar mount with squares at the side of the Mercury finger this will move them towards being dedicated students, writers, musicians, or even "dream analysts," a rather interesting and fulfilling occupation.

Knotty fingers are the greatest help to have for these Moon folk. All the airy-fairy stuff that floats around for them is turned into practical writers, deep thinkers, and excellent teachers. Smooth fingers are impulsive, intuitive, disliking detail and analysis. They bring their imagination into poetry, painting,

sculpture, and art of some form. They too, need to be held down to create or they will be constantly moving around, changing their ideas and their occupations. Creative indeed, but not too practical.

If the Moon mount is absent on the palm, there will be little or no visualization, just dense materialism. If the mount is elongated on a sensitive hand, watch for hypersensitivity. These people will take offense extremely quickly over the most trivial things.

Excessive development of the mount indicates a flighty, over-imaginative person, even the possibility of losing the mind – maybe eventual insanity – read this one very carefully. See if the thumb is short; if so, this will reduce both the will and the reason. This is the visionary, vacillating, weak person, especially if the thumb is also pointed. Other indications of an unbalanced mind will be shown by the Head line being broken, wavy, islanded, chained, poorly marked, or badly colored. If a star is also there, most likely there is a lack of mental concentration, a lack of firmness, a weak brain, too vivid an imagination, and continual vacilation.

It is an interesting observation that insanity – lunacy – (the Moon) shows up in full force when the Moon is full. Mental institutions and the police force are well aware of this fact and often have more staff on duty.

On a more pleasant note, when the Moon mount energies touch the finger mount of Jupiter, a great deal of creative imagination is shown. If the Saturn mount is also involved in this combination, it can produce an excellent dreamer who can spot patterns and trends in the economy while in the dream state. On the other side of the coin, this cleverness can create excessive self-absorption and an inflated idea of self importance.

If Saturn is involved with the Moon mount, often a mystical nature will come to the fore as Saturn has occult leanings and is inclined towards superstitions. If the Cross of Intuition is found near the Moon mount this will confirm the interest in psychic areas. The mount of the Moon is associated with emotions and the past. If a psychic hand is combined with these aspects there will be an active inner world, softening Saturn's often remote, cool nature. This will gradually lead into a combined interest in history, science, mysticism, and a fascination with the Noetic Sciences, dealing with the potential of collective conscious thought being able to affect matter. Saturn likes to deal with the depths of the mind. Confirmation will be shown by a rather nice deep pink color on the Moon mount.

The Moon leaning into the Mercury finger mount will bring inventive ideas. Cleverness and quick perception is shown if a triangle appears on the line between the two mounts the underlying deceptiveness of Mercury can produce very competent Private Investigators.

Mars Mounts

I have previously mentioned the Upper Mars mount and if you look at the diagram again you will note there is also a Lower Mars mount just above the Venus mount. Look again, and you will see a triangle shape in the middle of the palm between the lines of Life and Head. This is called the Plane of Mars, making three Mars mounts in all.

The natural nature of all three Mars mounts is aggressiveness of some sort in all areas of life, frequently in the mental or business world, fighting against adverse elements and circumstances. The aggressive and resistant qualities are essential to fill out and balance each type of person – not just a Martian type – without them, achievement is difficult. An absence of the Lower Mars mount, this shows little or no aggression, is indicative of failure by allowing other more inferior folk, to use their aggression to get the better of them and gain the position they were aiming for. You will need to look at all three mounts to see if there are deficiencies in any of them.

As I commented earlier, the Upper Mars mount is resistance. Cool and calm under all circumstances, rarely feeling discouraged, there is a great dislike of authority as there is a need of self-importance. This strong need shows itself if the Jupiter finger mount or the Apollo finger mount – or both – is activated by the Line of Achievement. Jupiter being the opportunist, there is a great desire to become a leader in his/her field. With Apollo, organizing leadership and self-assurance shows up along with a great deal of creativity. Mars, often referred to as the "battering ram" has plenty of initiative and tends to be somewhat belligerent. When the Mercury finger mount is activated there is a diversity of talents and the energy is frequently directed to satirical speech and cutting or abusive remarks when angered.

Look closely at the outer side of the hand – the percussion it is called. If that portion of the hand is flat or hollow, then the Upper Mars mount is absent. What a loss this is. This person is easily discouraged, lacks resistance and gives up quickly in the face of difficulties.

If the Plane of Mars in the center of the palm is over developed – (high), or it is crossed by fine or red lines, sudden outbursts of temper will take place. If a large single cross is also shown it indicates that the temper is uncontrollable. If the palm is hollow, there is a lack of temper. This is often shown in the hands of successful people, and the good clear Head Line that accompanies it gives self control and good judgment.

The Lower Mars mount is the really aggressive one. If this mount is fat and over developed this person will push forward with great persistence, resisting any attempts of being imposed on. Pushing, shoving over every obstacle, they just will not be beaten. There is little consideration for others as they intend to get what they have set their sights on, even when it comes to love affairs. Note that the Lower Mars mount sits just above the Venus mount and Venus can be equally as antagonistic if it is leaning upwards towards the Mars mount.

Venus

Venus is very much attracted to the opposite sex. The strong sexual/physical passions imbued within this mount can actually lead to perverted ideas if the hand itself is hard, plus a branch line from the Lower Mars ending in the mount of Luna area and the Venus mount is quite grilled. This shows a lack of moderation, possibly with a brutal, intemperate nature. If the Line of Life is also forked it can indicate a violent or vicious disposition and instability. If you come across these, look for a good fine Head Line as this will counteract a good deal of the negative indications, bring much self control and good judgment. If the thumb is also large, determination to control the over-passionate nature will help considerably.

Doesn't sound much like the kind, sweet loving Venus that is portrayed in portraits and stories does it? Like everything else, Venus has two sides to her nature and desires.

When we think of Venus, our minds automatically register love, sympathy, sensuality, tender passion. Being instinctively drawn to people by feelings of friendship and sympathy, these feelings often develop into love that is the primary Venus attribute. Venus never turns a deaf ear to the sufferings and woes of others, always ready to aid one way or another. Because of this generosity, warm heart and loving nature Venus is often taken advantage of by lesser human beings who have little or no morals, recognizing this nature as a "soft touch."

Venus is all of these and more on this side of her nature. One could say that beauty is her middle name for this mount is attracted to anything that stirs the electric currents of her emotions: flowers, colors, paintings, physical beauty, and especially music. Many have wonderful singing voices and musical talent.

The musician is portrayed by a good strong line from the Venus mount across to the line of the Apollo finger mount and the Mercury finger mount. If you see a good line of Head and smooth square fingers with conic, spatulate or square tips, this person could become a world-renowned musician. The ability to develop into an artist is here if there is a good strong line to the Apollo finger mount and the Apollo finger is the longest of the four. Writing, acting – they love parts that move the audience to tears – and with a strong line to the Saturn finger, they can become great comedians. Saturn's sense of humor can be quite droll.

In between the lower physical type of Venus and the lofty elevated one are different levels depending on the other mounts and finger phalanges involved. The lines and markings on the hand that also alter the basic reading come up in the next chapter.

The Venus mount reaching out to the Jupiter finger mount encourages ambition in their choice of field. The Saturn mount adds wisdom and clips the wings of the over exuberance of the sexy type, the Mercury mount adds shrewdness to bring a certain amount of success to the business dealings/affairs. With the Apollo mount, Venus doesn't get very far, as Apollo and Venus are too much alike loving beauty and pleasures. There is not much force to accomplish anything unless Saturn intervenes. Leaning towards the Lunar mount, Venus becomes self-indulgent, lazy, and over imaginative, and lying close to the base of the thumb, it becomes exceedingly emotional.

Out of the seven types, we have discussed Venus brings love, charm, passion, and beauty to the world, a wonderful package that we all appreciate.

The Principle Lines

Chapter 6

Now we come to the most interesting portion of palmistry – the lines on the hand. These indicate the psychological tendencies of the person in conjunction with the type of hand that has previously been defined. The type of person – hand – gives clues to the future in the way the individual psyche – the mind – reacts to the material world. The lines on the hand do change over a period of time due to the alteration in thinking patterns, lessons learned or not, through errors committed that rearrange the future for the individual. In a sense, the future is an extension of the present and what changes the life pattern and the lines on the hand is our thought power. Focusing strongly on various things, catapulting oneself into acting in certain ways by thought patterns bring about inner changes that reflect onto the outside world of the person. This then, creates the individual's own reality.

Whether you activate the Head line (mentality), the Heart line (emotions), you will alter the Saturn/Fate/Destiny line which, in turn, impinges on the Sun line and the Health line. All add up to an alteration of the Life line. The main lines of the hand are the original map of life and they fade and disappear as the mind changes over the various matters the lines indicate, then new lines take place showing new directions. What powerful minds we have that are so capable of controlling our circumstances, if only we are aware enough to recognize it.

Life Line

We will start our investigation with the Life Line. Look at the diagram of the hand (see Figure 1) and you will note that this line starts from the edge of the palm between the thumb and the index finger and curves down around the base of the thumb encircling the fleshy, puffy bit of the Mount of Venus.

This line shows the vitality and strength of the body. Where does it come from and how did it get there in that particular place? You will note that the line starts on or just under the Jupiter – index – finger which is the strongest finger on the hand. The energy from this finger passes upwards through the arm, continuing through and around the body, up through the spine activating the chakras then connecting to the mind. The mind controls and alters the lines of the hand through the strength of our thoughts. A rather neat magnetic current that flows continuously through and around us although we cannot see it. Nevertheless, we use it daily from the moment we are born when the Universal energy first flows into the Jupiter finger activating the life path.

The energy of this finger has been shown throughout history in many ways: beginning with word of mouth, then through many books including the various bibles and in the paintings of some of the great artists who use the finger to draw our attention to a point within the painting. We too, automatically use that finger as a pointer – the teacher points to a pupil with it, the winning sports person raises it in the air, when somebody feels they are being pushed or manipulated they say "get your finger out of my back." It's used in so many ways we are frequently unaware we use it. In its negative fashion, pointing it at another person it can be used as a curse drawing on the darker energies and a deep reservoir of emotions, it is also used to pull the trigger on a gun with the intention of killing. The light and dark energies that I talked about in my previous two books are at play here.

Another interesting feature, if you look at Figure 1 again, is how the Heart, Head, and Life lines all point towards Jupiter and that the times of events are read from under the Jupiter finger, across the palm for the Head and Heart lines and down the palm towards the wrist for the Life line. Here we see the metaphysical energies and the material world being joined together.

You will often find the beginnings of the Heart, Head, and Life lines are joined or very close together, but the Life line is the most important because it shows the vigor and natural health of the person. This line does not indicate death, that's shown on the Heart line, Head line, Mercury line (the line of health) and perhaps other lines like the worry lines, lines of Opposition, or the lines of Influence that produce illness if dwelt upon unnecessarily for any length of time.

The Lines of Influence are found just under the base of the thumb and the Venus mount indicating people who influence your life. If you get out your magnifying glass you'll be able to see them quite clearly and where they go. Lines right under the thumb represent family members, relatives, and friends. The line radiating from the Venus mount points to strangers entering your life who can be of help or lead you astray. It could also intimate an introduction to Ms. or Mr. Right. If the line reaches to the Life line, then the time shown on the Life line will indicate marriage. If there is a line appearing from the Moon mount reaching over to the Line of Destiny (Fate) at the same time, lining up with the time on the Life line, here you have corroboration of the event. Lines running parallel to the Life line show helping hands and support, often from parents – the closer to the Life line, the greater the help.

Lines under the thumb ending before the Life line are indicative of being able to choose ones own social relationships without interference. But if the line crosses over and cuts into the Destiny line, there will be much interference from family members and parents over career choice, business matters, social relationships, and marriage partner. This control over the life of a person can be quite detrimental to one who is of a sensitive nature and totally unfitted for the life that has been chosen for him/her. If the mount of Venus is low on the hand a great deal of overwhelming irritation will be felt eventually leading to dire action being taken. A line of escape from these controls will be shown by a single long line from the Mount of Venus extending across the palm to the area of the Moon. This escape line will be utilized by way of running away from responsibilities, indulging in drugs, sexual perversion, or any other way of getting out from under the control of other people. If the ends of the lines are frayed this magnifies the situation, possibly leading to suicide. Check out the thumb; if it is short there is a lack of will power, if it is also small the character is weak and help should be given before the step of suicide is taken. Here you can see why the information learned about the thumb in Chapter Two is so important.

Look again at the Life line, if it is deep and shows well, there is plenty of strength and vigor, probably few illnesses in life and the body able to resist disease. People with this strong line are usually very self-confident and they are frequently an inspiration to others.

On the contrary, a narrow thin line indicates less vitality and resistance to illness, and likely to have a number of health problems throughout life.

The Life line usually starts just under the mount of Jupiter. If it starts actually on the mount itself, you can read this as being an extremely ambitious person. Providing there is a strong thumb and Head line to back up the ambition, then success is a given within the chosen goals. The other side of the coin with this success is the Jupiterian tendency to eat, drink, and be merry as I mentioned in the description of the Jupiter person. If the Life line is on the thin side coming from the Jupiter mount, this will be of benefit, reducing the tendency to over indulge. They may be a little bit on the nervous side but the benefit of the thin line for them is the avoidance of apoplexy and blood disorders which undoubtedly comes from excess.

To get closer to accuracy, the Life, Head, and Heart lines should also be considered together before judgment. If the Life line joins the Head Line, here is a thinking person, cautious, carrying out constructive planning. If they are slightly separated there will be a highly energetic nature, but a wide separation shouts of impulsiveness and a tendency to make hasty and frequently unwise decisions. If you are looking at the hand of a child and see that the Life line and the Head lines are joined for quite some distance along the palm, the child is likely to be shy or timid in the early years of childhood. The parents should be advised to give the child extra encouragement to help develop self-confidence.

Apart from the timing of events and the state of vitality, vigor, and constitution, what else can the Life line tell us? A bunch of ascending branches from the Life line – they look like little feathers – ending under the first finger, is a sign of a great desire for wealth and power – most definitely a Jupiter influence. If the branches drop down inside the Life line towards the thumb there is a great desire and craving for the love and affection.

Swinging over to the far side of the palm towards the mount of the Moon you will need to add the imagination and adventurous aspects to the Life line reading. This entails lots of travel, different occupations that vary from time to time demanding constant change. There is a love of travel, and if the Head line is also strong there will be a lot of restlessness. If the Headline droops towards the Moon mount, it indicates the imagination and creative faculties of the artist, musician, writer, designer, etc.

If this Life line has a line branching off to and under the Saturn finger, this person prefers solitude and may also be deeply religious. If this branch line starts inside the Life line on the Venus mount, domestic and personal grievances and unfairness cause a lot of unhappiness in life.

A straight line from the Life line running up to Apollo – the third finger – there is usually a lot of help from friends and family, frequently resulting in either wealth or fame. This *must* be a straight line – wavy or broken lines show struggles that more than likely are a hindrance towards attaining the ultimate goal.

If there is a connecting line to Mercury – the little finger – that is as strong as the Life line and there are no breaks in it, there will be success in business or profession and material well-being usually with the help of loved ones. But, if this line cuts through a strong Destiny or Apollo line, it shows interference in business projects – maybe too many people interested in the same things or have the same ideas. The end result is a dubious business outcome.

These small lines that cut through the Life line are often called "bad luck" lines because they hinder business or inflict unhappiness here and there along the life path. They are annoying interferences that may be found on any of the lines demanding different interpretations and where they terminate is important.

Chained formations, a forked end or broken lines on the Life line warn of physical weakness. Check both palms. On the minor, left hand, if there are still any showing it would point to childhood ailments which are to be expected. Appearing on the dominant right hand, count the time on the line and you can see if the illness or physical weakness has passed or is still to come at a certain time in the future. A cross formation indicates a threat of ill health late in life. Knowing the time in advance it could be averted. You'll learn how to count time in Chapter Eight.

A double Life line, sometimes called a sister line, either complete or partial, gives extra strength to the body so any breaks in this main line are protected from the danger of serious illness or the danger is either lessened or prevented. A square on the Life line is also a mark of preservation.

As you will have noticed, other lines on the hand interact with whichever line you are working with. No line stands or works alone, and in most cases, you will find the thumb interpretations need to be added to flesh out the information you have come across.

Head Line

Let us move on now to the Line of Head which indicates the intellect, the strength of the mental powers and physical strength of the brain. The better color and more even the line the better is the concentration of the mind, the self control and less danger of brain disorders. Note very carefully if the Head line has lots of little islands and hairlines. This points to much pain in the head and very possibly brain disease.

The Head line starts on the same side as the Life line – usually just above it – between the thumb and the index finger. It goes across the palm, sloping gently downwards ending either on the mount of Mars or on the upper part of the mount of the Moon. If this line makes a rapid downward approach into the mount of the Moon, there could be a vivid imagination with much artistic ability varying towards an excess of imagination leading to day-dreaming and a most impractical attitude towards daily affairs. If there is a fork on the line terminating on the mount of the Moon, it promises imaginative literary talent. When the Headline curves into the mount of Mars – above the Moon mount – this shows a successful business life. This person has a keen sense of the value of money and it will accumulate rapidly, but beware, here is a hard task master towards employees.

As I mentioned earlier at the beginning of the book, both hands should be consulted. Now is the time to have a good look and compare what the subconscious from the left hand indicated and what the conscious mind of the right hand is now producing. You can see what modifications have taken place between the two hands as a child grew to become an adult and how the force of the mind altered the life map modifying the original qualities shown in the left hand.

Looking at the left hand, the Head line is often slightly joined to the Life line at the start of life and then branches away. This join registers the early years of life and the earlier the detachment of Head and Life lines the younger the person was in taking control and starting to think for him/her self.

A long, clear and straight line reveals a thoughtful, calculative type of mind. Free from islands, line formations, etc., it gives the ability to concentrate without being interrupted by anxieties or apprehensions. The long line gives a wide scope of understanding while the shorter line means the mental comprehension is more restricted. If the line is short in the left hand and has become long in the right, then the mentality has been developed. If the Head line is longer in the left hand and short in the right, then mental retrogradation has taken place – possibly through an accident or it may be pointing to danger of an accident or a fatality. If the line is broken in two under the mount of Saturn, this confirms an early sudden death, but if a square is also found along the broken line, this person could be saved from an accident, or even violence, through courage or presence of mind. If the line is abnormally short it forewarns of an early death from some mental affection.

The wider the space at its beginning from the Life line indicates a restlessness and a desire for constant change and variety, a line from the mount of the Moon to the Head line will back this up. Sometimes the Head line starts on the line of Mars which is just inside the Life line and above the mount of Venus on the thumb. With the start making such a wide separation it does not augur well. This person is sensitive, nervous, usually quite irritable and frequently battling with neighbors. Vacillating in thought and action, the temperament is inclined to be fretful, always finding something to worry about, yet willing to take chances without sufficient thought of the consequences.

If the Head line has a pronounced upward bulge beneath one of the finger mounts or actually on the base of the finger, the intellect will be influenced by that particular mount. For instance, a bulge rising under the second finger suggests the Saturnian characteristics of prudence, wisdom, discretion, and shrewdness will have an effect on the mind. Under the fourth finger beneath Mercury, this indicates a certain amount of tact, but as Mercury is very sharp witted, it could lead to double dealing. Under Jupiter, ambition and pride steps forth with a great desire for power and if the line from the Head line to this Jupiter area is strong and deep success will take place.

If you see triangles on the line of Head on either or both hands then this person is acquiring new intellectual skills. Triangles correspond to pleasurable influences often linked with learning and the position on the line of Head will indicate the subject of interest. Beneath the mount of Saturn it points to history and other Saturnian interests, under the Sun mount, arts and pleasures and under the Mercury mount, language or other forms of communication. With the triangle on the mount or beneath the finger of Jupiter there may well be a management course taken at that time (shown on the time line) to increase organizational skills, executive ability and management of people leading to eventual success and recognized status in society. All these intellectual decisions that have come to light are rooted in the subconscious and are ultimately connected to the emotional energies pointing to a connection of the Head and Heart lines. Here you can decide if the person is ruled by the head or the emotions or whether they are neatly balanced.

A further indication to help guide your decision is that the line should only reach to the area of Apollo or just to Mercury but not extending to the edge of the palm. This is an excellent Head line representing mental balance and power, intellectual ability and a good memory, leaning more towards being lead by the head than by the emotions. If the line is very short there is likely to be a lack of ambition or not enough energy to fulfill any ambition if there is one at all.

Small lines that join the Head and Life lines at the beginning indicate that the person is forced into a living contrary to his/her plans or desires. We discussed some of this with the lines of Interference, this gives some back up of this problem. If the Head line is abnormally long, extending right to the edge of the palm this denotes a secretive, selfish person who is very demanding of others. The Heart line joining the Head line to make one path shows a cool, calculating person, ruled totally by Head, not allowing emotions any way in. You will note that many of these indications are in line and fit neatly with the descriptions of the type of person discussed in earlier chapters.

There are many other formations, irregularities, and signs indicated on the lines such as crosses, circles, grilles, forked or tasseled lines, sister lines, branches and so on that I will cover in more detail in Chapter Nine. For now, we will move onto the Heart line and see how it connects to other areas of the hand.

Heart Line

The Heart line is the key to the emotional and passionate side our nature. It is indicative of how we feel – how we utilize our emotions. In other words do we allow them to run riot, out of control, upsetting our life style and that of others, or are they controlled and reasonably well balanced.

The Heart line is situated just above the Head line. It also starts from beneath the Jupiter finger or between the Jupiter and Saturn fingers. It usually takes a dip downwards across the palm, then rises again towards the base of Mercury or finishing between Mercury and the mount of Mars (just above the Moon mount).

If the Heart, Head, and Life lines – the three major lines in the hand – are joined at the start, we have an extremist here – one who is irrational or unreasonable in affections and family life. This lack of good judgment causes unhappiness and disappointments, unless it is contradicted by a forked formation at the beginning. This fork eventually leads to a nicely well balanced home life. On the contrary, if that forked formation is at the end of the line then there is a danger of separation ending in divorce.

A clear line right across the palm is indicative of a love of family, plus a great deal of sympathy for others, but if the line starts high, under the base of

Jupiter, although the nature is warm and affectionate, jealousy lurks underneath. Starting low on the hand, close to the line of Head, the Heart line shows that the emotions welling up from the subconscious will always take precedence and interfere with the logical or practical affairs of the head.

There are other interesting features of note on the Heart line. If an island appears on the line it sometimes signifies an impending event. Look back on the line to see if there has been a sudden swerve of the Head line upwards to Jupiter suggesting a sudden, intense, passionate love affair, especially later in life. If the island has appeared along with a line descending from the Heart line to the Head line, then it is likely that an engagement will be broken off before the date of marriage. A break or branch in the line under Saturn confirms the broken engagement and that the warnings of prudence from Saturn have gone unheeded. If there is also a break under Apollo at the same time, this says that it is a lucky break for this mismatched couple.

A line from the Heart line to the Life line points to a disappointment of some sort and the possible loss of a family member bringing on sorrow. A chance line moving into the Mercury area says someone has extravagant tastes. Either a family member or a loved one could well be the cause of business failure. Money matters must be taken into consideration. On the other hand, a line ascending to Apollo indicates that too much attention being given to career is interfering with home life that could lead to problems.

With wavy lines on the Heart line there will always be uncertainty in love and if it is also chained there is difficulty in making choices. Circles on the line point to misunderstandings and final separations, and crosses are usually some indication of money matters such as debts and over spending as the emotions of the "I Want Syndrome" have encouraged the unnecessary outlay of money.

Fate Line (Destiny/Saturn)

Now let's look at the Fate line – the line of Destiny/Saturn – that runs from the base of the palm near the wrist sometimes in a straight line upwards to the mount of Saturn under the second finger. Going straight up onto the mount of Saturn is a sign of extremely good fortune and great success. This line on the left hand (the right hand if you are left handed) is your destiny and the line on the right hand shows how you have taken control of your life within the boundary that maps our lives.

Instead of going straight up the palm to Saturn, the line may end on Jupiter or bend towards the Apollo mount. In either case the destiny will be influenced by the qualities of the mount. Ending on Jupiter there is the promise of a very successful career with some unusual distinction and power gained purely through putting energy, ambition, and determination to work. Bending towards Apollo, it offers success in literary or artistic enterprises, once again by grasping opportunities as they arise and putting willpower and determination to work to achieve the desired ends. After all, determination is only a force that pushes something else and it must have something push – to accomplish. So if you have a strong desire to paint, write, play an instrument – anything that appeals strongly to you, then do it. Put your willpower into it and determination will bring about the success. This line of Destiny is cause and effect – think about it – when you kick the ball of cause the effect will come your way.

When you read the Line of Fate/Destiny/Saturn, it will reveal the route, the goal and the destiny proposed by the left (minor) hand. It mirrors our lives briefly and to the point, far more than the other lines, due to the changes we constantly make with our decisions creating our own reality. This hand shows the basic tendencies and past events. The right hand shows how these tendencies change and develop and what is to come through the traits we have and implement satisfactorily or with dire results.

Whereas the Line of Life reflects the timing of bodily changes (physically, mentally, and emotionally every seven years) and family influences or interferences, the line of Fate indicates times of change of direction – a total career change, a job change, set backs, triumphs, for this line is concerned solely with material success.

In some hands you will see that no line of Destiny is apparent – yet the owner of the hands is a very successful and wealthy person. Here you see the "self-made man" who has made use of all energies and opportunities, put willpower and determination to work and has achieved the desired success through his/her own efforts. Then again, this line can rise directly from the bottom center of the palm indicating the same thing – success largely through the person's own efforts. Rising inside the Life line and curving up to the finger of Saturn, once more it indicates material success in life, this time with the help of close relatives. Another place the line can rise from is the mount of the Moon – on the percussion side of the hand, opposite the thumb. Success in life will be aided and assisted by a member of the opposite sex with either money or good advice. This could also indicate a person who rises to fame in the eye of the public and is handled by an agent or a person who guides in the life in a beneficent manner.

Our worldly success can be dependent on people who influence us in a beneficial or detrimental way and to the barriers and obstacles that stand in the way and how they are overcome. The timing on this Destiny line starts at the wrist area. If the line is quite low and attached or very close to the Life line, the wishes of the parents and relatives have been imposed on this person. As the lines separate you will see the age the individual has been able to take control of his/her own destiny – if at all. Recall the Life line cutting into the Destiny line indicating interference? Note the diagram of the time lines blocked on it into years of seven where you can judge the timing of events. More about time later on in Chapter Eight.

If the Destiny line runs right up the palm, over the mount into the finger of Saturn it would seem that people suddenly turn against this individual bringing on his/her downfall, possibly because of the inner attitude and the lack of adaptability to the changing world. If the line is chained, adaptability is uneven, the person is not happy, has feelings of uncertainty leading to frustration.

When the Destiny line stops abruptly at the line of Head on its upward journey, obstacles appear that prevent success from taking place. This is usually caused by a lack of thinking clearly, an over reaction, hasty move, or some stupidity.

If the Heart line intervenes, emotions, and affections can have a detrimental effect on success but if the Heart and Saturn lines join together and move up and over to join the Jupiter mount, the highest ambition of this person will be achieved through the affections.

When the Destiny line starts midway up the palm in the Plane of Mars, difficulties and troubles are encountered throughout life. If the line continues well up the hand they will be overcome after the first half of life is over. Success may come if through perseverance and determination they are put to work.

The Destiny line rising from the line of Head indicates success late in life providing there are no cutting lines or islands. If there are, then impediments and financial losses are indicated unless a square appears to protect and avert any disasters. Squares are usually protective signs. If you find one just touching the Plane of Mars but on the side of the Life line it foretells of an accident or danger within the home. If the square is on the other side of the Destiny line next to the mount of the Moon, a travel accident is indicated and a gentle warning should be given to the client.

When a break in the line appears on its upward trend it denotes misfortune and loss but if another line branches out just before the break it shows a complete change in life which is more pleasing to the person.

A double or "sister" Fate line is an excellent sign and they are surprisingly common on the hand. It shows two distinct careers and become important if they go to two separate mounts indicating success in both areas. It also lessens any misfortune shown from a break in the line.

Studying all the indications on or around the Destiny line and the marks and lines that enhance or detract will point to the direction and purpose in life. Dividing the time line of fate into sevens will be of great assistance in deciding when the changes of the destiny pattern will take place.

Sun Line (Apollo)

Now we come to the last of the principle lines – the Sun line or line of Apollo, often called the line of Success. Like the Destiny line, it normally starts at the base of the palm, running up into the ring finger – the third finger on the hand. The timing of events is also read from the bottom starting at zero – birth – and continuing on in seven year intervals until death intervenes. Where the line first appears on the hand is the time/age when this line of Sun begins to influence the individual.

Starting at the wrist and continuing in a straight line usually means a person is a quick thinker, is generally popular – possibly famous in the eye of the public. If the Apollo line ends in a star or a triangle on or near the mount of Apollo public recognition of his/her talent and fame and fortune are virtually guaranteed. If there is a square on this line, it will protect the public idol from any scandal and adversities that happen, as they will at various times in life.

If the Head line is exceptionally straight and connects to the Apollo line there will be a strong desire for a social position with power and to make as much money as possible. The Fate line will indicate where this person's interest lies.

At the other end of the scale, if the Apollo line starts between the Head and Heart lines and then peters out into a fork, a split or a faintly marked manner, this person's career will not be very profitable in the early years and practically non existent in later life. Not much of a satisfactory life at all.

If the line rises only from the Head line then the second half of life will be more productive having overcome obstacles caused by family or business. Well organized, self planned ideas, personal cleverness and dexterity in the areas of inventing appliances or mechanical devices could well bring financial security.

Rising from and joined to the Life line, the talents this person has will need to be encouraged and developed by some sort of organization or sponsored or financed by friends or family.

When the Apollo line starts from the area of the Moon a career of the imaginative type is likely to be chosen. Is the hand the conic, philosophic or psychic type? Musicians, composers, dancers, writers, actors, painters, architects and other creative people invariably have this line, and if the line ends close to the Mercury area beneath the little finger, business acumen and a materialistic attitude is combined with the creativity. Lucky people who also have that business mind.

This line of Apollo is not purely concerned with the artistic side of life. Combined with what has been noted from the Destiny line, look at the phalanges of the Apollo fingers and the thumb along with the type of hand. This will guide your decision as to whether this person's proper world lies in the mental, practical or in material matters. No doubt you will see some areas pointing to art, but it could be a business person who owns an art gallery, or a philanthropist who donates money to literary or art schools to help students, to an operatic society, the theatre or is a board member of organizations of an artistic leanings. This type of person is likely to have the square or spatulate hand.

When the Apollo line ends in a fork there will be more than one talent. And the person is very capable of successfully using both. If there is a triple fork – which is unusual – it gives a remarkable ability to gain wealth and fame. One side of the fork points towards Saturn's carefulness and the other to the shrewd instinct of Mercury giving permanence to Apollo's great talent.

The joining of the Apollo line to the Fate line indicates a partnership and a small line from Apollo just touching the Heart line brings a happy love affair that could end in marriage. But – that same line cutting through the Heart line points to a broken love affair and unhappiness.

If a cross is at the end of the Apollo line and leaning towards Saturn, this person is having serious thoughts about his/her career and personal life and may even be getting caught up in some sort of religious fervor.

Finally, to complete this chapter and move into the secondary (minor) lines, see if there is a broken line at the end of the Apollo line. This shows various periods of success with many different types of interest. These could be brought about by changes due to marriage, surroundings, ill health, or perhaps causes that are actually beyond this person's control. If there happens to be dots on the Apollo line, they are a menace to the reputation – small ones are whispers and gossip behind this person's back, but if they are large and deep there is a loss of the good name. When the Apollo line ends in just one dot there will be a loss of both reputation and money.

On a happy note, if the Apollo line has a double star this shows great fame and brilliancy. The position of the first star will show the age of the attainment of the first success and a star at the end shows that it will continue to the end of life.

The
Secondary
Lines

Chapter 7

The Secondary lines are often referred to as the Minor lines; some of them are quite useful, such as the Line of Mercury and the Girdle of Venus. Others are simply interesting.

Line of Mercury

The first of our minor lines that we shall investigate is the Line of Mercury because it deals with the patterns of our health.

It is interesting that Mercury should be named the Health line, Mercury being the planet of the mind. It is the way we think and how we apply those thoughts that alters the cellular structure of our bodies. We can bring an illness on ourselves quite easily with negative thoughts – feeling sorry for ourselves and dwelling on it, having a bad attitude towards the rest of the world which means solitude and no friends. Narrow mindedness eventually narrows the heart arteries leading to heart problems. Even positive self-centered thoughts lead to health problems – enjoying the constant round of parties, the over abundance of food and drink, late nights, and noisy clubs. Overdoing leads to liver conditions, biliousness, apoplexy – you will recall we talked about the Jupiterian type person who is prone to these diseases and the Saturn and Apollo types who have their own health problems. Ill health is frequently responsible for the failure of business or career or one's destiny choice and the culprit is the badly regulated liver and bile that clogs the brain, altering the thinking patterns.

The line of Mercury starts just above the wrist, somewhat towards the mount of the Moon, then moving up the palm at an angle towards the Mercury mount. If there isn't one there, don't worry, it's a favorable indication. This hand probably has few lines on it indicating a person who is not afflicted by nervousness. If a person lives on his/her nerves, this also affects the liver – a most important organ of the body.

The Mercury line should be deep. If so, it says this person has good vitality, a strong constitution, a healthy liver and an active clear brain and memory. This is what the line says if there are no other indications of defects coming from the principle lines. So if the hand shows strong Life, Head, Heart and Mars lines with the deep Mercury line, this person will have healthy days all through life.

If the Mercury line starts on or touches the Life line there is a weakness in the composition of the body suggesting a disease of some sort.

Rising from the line of Heart suggests a weakness of the heart and if the line is pale in color, bad circulation is indicated. Little red spots on the Mercury line are symptomatic of bouts of fever and when the line is wavy, look for biliousness and liver complaints like malaria and jaundice. The line in little broken pieces speaks of bad digestion and health impairments occurring at the time of the break. (Count along the time line). Islands point to lung, chest and throat problems.

When the line is chained, periods of ill health occur, with occasional hospital visits, the time of these you can estimate on the time line. Remember, too, that squares are always good, so when or where you see one, these will form some sort of protection and reduce the intensity of any one of these maladies.

When the Mercury line points to ill health of some sort, direct your attention first to the type of person you have delineated from your previous information. This will give you an indication of what's to come when you read the time line, consult the Head line, too, as this will give you further information. With the types, the Jupiterian folk suffer from gout, bronchitis, and pneumonia. The Saturnian from rheumatism and gout, the Apollonian from heart disturbances. The Mercurian suffers from indigestion, nerves, and the liver, the Martian has intestinal inflammation and appendicitis and the Moon type suffers from gout and rheumatism.

All in all, the Mercury line should be consulted together with the Life, Head, Heart and Apollo lines in combination with the type. Rather like a jig saw puzzle, when you have fitted in the right pieces the picture becomes evident. So it is with palm reading.

Girdle of Venus

Our next stop on the Secondary lines is the Girdle of Venus which I mentioned briefly some while back. The girdle usually runs in a half circle from beneath the Jupiter finger and can go as far across the palm to end up at the Mercury mount, and sometimes ending right on the percussion (the outside portion of the hand).

The main feature of the girdle is an intensity of nervousness and a highly sensitive nature. If the girdle is totally unbroken there is a tendency towards hysteria and depression. Along with this highly strung temperament are quick mood changes. One moment they are totally enthusiastic over something and the next moment down in the dumps and miserable. They are hard to live with and very exacting. If the girdle goes right over the edge of the hand and makes contact with the lines of Marriage, they can spoil it with their up and down temperament. Even a small slight or a feeling of inattention can make them "fly off the handle" causing a great deal of unhappiness to all and sundry.

What causes these problems? If you recall, I mentioned that the Jupiter finger was the strongest on the hand. This is where the electromagnetic current of the Universe first enters into our bodies. It then circulates throughout this temple of the Soul into every fiber of our being – it is often referred to as the

White Light. This Girdle of Venus causes a barrier to be erected against this White Light so it cannot circulate as it should from the Jupiter finger down through the Life line, traveling up to the brain, then returning through the lines of Saturn, Apollo and Mercury. This barrier causes the current of this light to overflow making new channels for itself wherever it can, intensifying every nerve it touches, leaving behind a highly nervous person and intense nervous activity.

Now, if the hand has only a few lines on the palm, the girdle is not so important as the one that has a myriad of fine lines. Feel the hand. If the texture is coarse and the mount of Venus is red and swollen, there may be wanton and lustful tendencies which consume the person's thinking patterns. These should be confirmed through the previous character analysis. The girdle can be very sensual, passionate, with a strong appetite for physical sexual indulgence. In a very nervous hand combined with a weak physical body, the sexual desire will show up in dreams of passionate intercourse.

If the Head line slopes into the mount of the Moon and at the end of the line there is a dot, cross or island along with a broken girdle of Venus plus many fine lines in the hand, this is a sign of possible insanity due to intense nervousness and intense imagination. Is there a broken girdle, a cross on the mount of Saturn, dots or islands on the Head line directly under Saturn plus a grille on the mount of the Moon? Paralysis is likely to overtake this person sometime in the life.

There are two sides to the girdle – broken lines indicate the nervous condition but a deeply grooved girdle line points to an excessive side that often ruins family life and friendships with the constant demands the person makes on others. If you do come up against a Girdle of Venus, study it carefully before making final decisions.

Line of Mars

Up next is the line of Mars situated inside the Life line close beside it. These two are "sister" lines and when the Mars line is very close to the Life line it will give added strength to the constitution, particularly with all square or broad hands. These are often found on the hands of soldiers. There are many quarrels and annoyances for this type bringing fighting qualities into play. Consequently, if the Life line is deep and the Mars line strong, there is great strength and vitality and unusual physical stamina. As with all Martian indications, there is aggression and a fighting spirit so there needs to be a creative outlet of some sort to use up the vitality, otherwise the energy will be dispersed in eating, drinking, and drunken fights depending on the type of character. If the mount of Venus is large and the Life line and Mars line are strong there is an excessive sexual appetite. If the Mars line cuts the lines of Saturn or Apollo, this will have a dire effect on the career.

If a branch line shoots out from the Mars line to the mount of the Moon, there is a craving for excitement and the nature is likely to be brutal and intemperate. When a star also shows up on this branch line it confirms the lack of control and a forked ending points to violence and a vicious disposition. A cross, dot or bar at the end indicates a sudden death from the excesses of life.

A very long line of Mars gives a remarkably active life with the subject ending life far from the original birth place. People in the military or the police are frequently endowed with this line. The short line indicates unusual bravery and gives physical aid and energy when strain or nervous pressure seems to be almost unbearable.

Interestingly, despite the Mars line being made of "fighting stuff," if it appears only on the left hand – the subconscious hand – the owner has a great imagination and most likely psychic abilities.

The Via Lascivia

The fourth line we will look at is called the Via Lascivia. It is not often seen, but when it appears on the hand it is a "sister" line to the line of Mercury that we've already covered. It rises from the inside of the mount of the Moon, running beside the Mercury line towards the percussion side of the hand. If the Mercury line is weak, this will give added strength and the physical stamina to overcome any defects of the Mercury line.

When this line is on both hands and completely parallel to the Mercury line, there is a lust for money and a highly developed appetite for sexual pleasure. Starting from the line of Life it tends towards an immoral life, a wavy line speaks of a fickle person and a chained line is carnal and wanton. Perhaps it is a good thing it is not often seen on the hand!

A branch line from the Via Lascivia crossing over the Mercury line and just touching a line of Apollo there is unexpected wealth giving luxurious living, but should a star be on the Lascivia then this wealth will be easily squandered on friends, high and foolish living, and gambling.

If the Lascivia and Mercury lines are equally strong there will be two successful careers. On a woman's hand, she will have a business career as well as her home and family.

Looking at the lines of Opposition, these are horizontal lines on the mount of Upper Mars – just above the mount of the Moon. These represent opposing other people either in the way of finances or some personal affair that ends up in enmity. The lines are usually short, running towards the line of Heart.

If these lines are unusually short there are many unimportant quarrels to deal with plus a lot friction – irritating more than anything else. If the lines are long, reaching across to the Life line or the mount of Venus, serious family problems interfere with life.

The lines reaching either the line of Apollo or Saturn indicates a threat or danger of a lawsuit. If the owner of the hand has a long thumb and a strong Head line, the oppositions involve lawyers, judges, or appointees of the court connected with the law who handle the problems. If these lines cut into the Heart line, the affections are involved – possibly a divorce or custody action.

One good thing here – when the lines curve up and end on the area of Apollo, this is a lucky turn. Despite opposition from a variety of other people, there will be a most successful career purely due to personal effort.

Travel Lines

The end of the Secondary lines for us is the Travel lines. These can be found by the mount of the Moon, just on the edge of the palm opposite the mount of Venus. If there are many lines there is a great restlessness and a lot of trips will be taken for both business and pleasure. If the lines are deep, these represent important journeys. Starting at the percussion side of the hand, the travel will be by sea and air. If the lines are on the actual area of the mount of the Moon then travel will be mainly by land.

When a journey line ends in a cross, the journey brings some disappointment. If there is a square on the travel line it points to danger, but the traveler will be protected. When there is an island there, the journey presages loss.

The line running across to the mount of Saturn indicates a fatality of some sort on the journey and if the line runs into the Head line causing a break, spot or island, some danger to the head is threatened or some sickness is indicated.

If the travel line crosses the hand into the mount of Jupiter, this will be an extremely long journey but some position of power will be gained at journey's end. When the horizontal lines on the actual mount of the Moon reach across to the Destiny line, this also will be a long and important journey. When the lines touch the line of Fate and move upwards with it there is material benefit to be gained from the journey.

The travel line reaching the Apollo mount seems to bring fame and money, and reaching to the mount of Mercury sudden and unexpected wealth appears.

Any time these horizontal lines curve downwards towards the wrist, an unfortunate journey takes place, but rising upwards they will always be successful.

So where will people go on their journeys or vacations? At the beginning of the book I mentioned the four elements of Fire, Earth, Air, and Water. These have a distinct association with the types of people and they fit very nicely with their hands in connection with travel and their choices. Providing there are no other indications in the palm to alter their views these are likely to be their choices.

Fire hands

have the oblong palm and short fingers and are the adventurous type. Give them the opportunity and they'll explore new places at any time.

Earth hands

have square hands and short fingers and like to return to the same place on their vacations rather than take a chance on the unknown.

Air hands

with square palms and long fingers just love to travel. They frequently pursue a career in the travel industry just so they can travel. The job in the office is not for them.

Water hands

with the oblong palms (longer than wide) and long fingers often choose to travel to the mystical and spiritual places. They are also enchanted by places of intrigue and the mysterious.

Great Triangle and Quadrangle

To wrap up this chapter, I would like to introduce you to the Great Triangle and the Quadrangle that you will find in the center of the palm, the triangle being formed by the lines of Life, Head and the Mercury line.

If you look at the diagram of the mounts of the hand, you will see the triangle that contains the Plane of Mars and above it the Quadrangle between the lines of Head and Heart.

The line of Mercury that forms the base of the triangle is frequently missing so the line of Apollo will take its place and form the base. This Apollo line shows great individuality encouraging power and success yet it detracts from the broad-mindedness that the Mercury line would give.

When the triangle is well formed with the Mercury line there are liberal beliefs and opinions and a generosity of heart. If the triangle lines tend to be

wavy, then the person is inclined towards cowardice, timidity, and meanness.

The point of the triangle should have two clear even points giving a good mind and clarity of thought. If the points are rounded the intellect tends to be dull, and if the points are far apart and wide there is a hasty temper, impatience continually offending people.

A good line of health – the Mercury line – to the Head line gives good health, a quick mind, and a vivacious personality. If the Mercury line is pointed, the health is not too good and the temperament is nervous. If the line is blunt or rounded at the end the person tends towards stupidity. A cross in the triangle denotes an active person and many lines forming a grille says the person is very argumentative.

The Quadrangle is the space between the Head and Heart lines. It should be wide at both ends with few markings showing a powerful intellect and being a good loyal friend.

When the area is narrow, there is a narrowness of thought, bigotry, jealousy, and pettiness. If it narrows in the center giving a "waist-like" appearance, there will be prejudice and injustice as well, yet the person will be very concerned about the opinions other people hold about him/her.

If the quadrangle is very wide, the subject is independent, very selfish, and somewhat perverse, and cross lines give irritability and nervousness.

A star anywhere in the quadrangle is a good sign of success. Near the Jupiter end it indicates power and pride, near Saturn success in choice of career, near Apollo success in some art form and at the end between Apollo and Mercury success in scientific matters or research.

Time on Your Hands

Chapter 8

Figure 6:
Time on Lines of Life, Head, and Heart

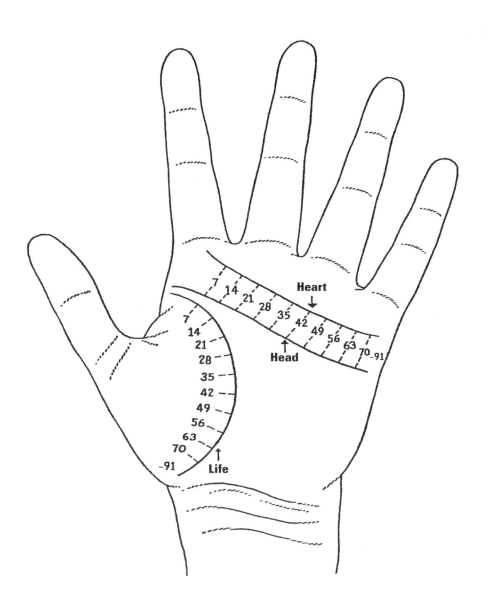

Figure 7:
Time on the Lines

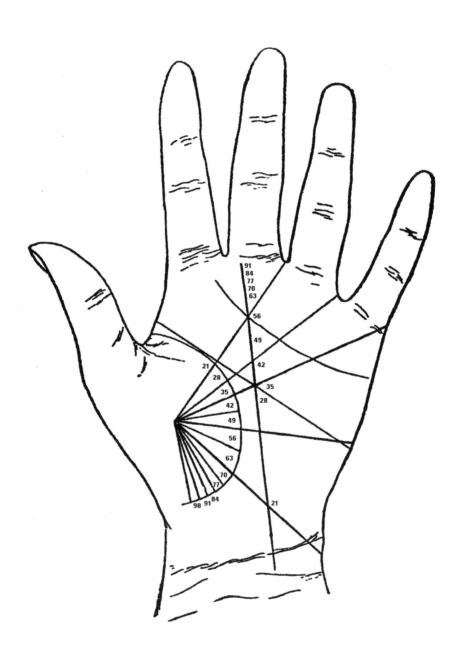

Past, present, and future – there they are, written in the palms of your hands. Marking off the major lines in periods of sevens show, more or less, when events took place in the past, what is happening at the present time and seeing what is coming up in the future from the lines just forming in the right hand.

Why must it be in sevens you ask? It doesn't necessarily. Some palmists use five-year markings, others use six-year demarcations. It just makes sense to me to use seven-year segments as all the cells in our bodies are renewed at roughly seven-year intervals. The movement of the planets in astrology show their seven-year movements indicating growth and events taking place. Witness, for instance, Saturn's seven-year movement: Around the age of seven, a child is learning, beginning to take control of him/herself and the surroundings. About the age of fourteen, puberty takes place along with some responsibility. For Jewish boys it is a year earlier. At the twenty-first birthday, there is acceptance into the world as an adult. During the next seven years, marriage frequently takes place; by thirty-five years, there is career achievement. At forty-two to forty-nine, men experience the male menopause; forty-nine to fifty-six, women experience the same thing. At sixty-three, the eye is on retirement, pension, freedom of restriction from the work place and responsibilities, and so the sevens continue on with one's own choice of the remaining life pattern until death releases us. The planets Uranus, Neptune, and Pluto have also been moving through the planetary system during this time at their own rate of speed, and at age fifty-six, all three planets plus Saturn come together impressing the more spiritual energies of the Universe on mind and body. So much seems to rely on the number seven which is why I prefer to time the events with it.

Looking at the time Figure 6 you will see the Life line is timed from just above the thumb running around in a half circle from zero years to seven to fourteen on to ninety-one years. People seem to be living longer these days. Now the Heart line and the Head lines run across the palm from the Jupiter side to the percussion – the outer side of the palm, again starting from zero to ninety-one years. The other major lines – Destiny (Fate), Apollo and Mercury start at the bottom of the hand by the wrist and rascettes (rings between the palm and wrist), moving upwards to the fingers, zero to ninety-one years again. You will notice the Mercury line is at an angle starting from just outside the Life line but the spaces on this line between the years will be closer together as the Mercury line is shorter than the others. In judging where these time divisions will come on the hand, you will have to decide whether the hand is long or short. A long hand will have wider spacing between the years to be marked and a short hand will have them closer.

Tip!

An excellent way to read the palms is to photograph both hands. Use a digital camera; put them into your computer then you can make a big enlargement and print it out. You can draw the lines on the print and put in the years and you'll find it much easier to read with more accuracy than reading the actual palm.

You must read both hands now – the left hand shows the original map of life and the right hand shows how the person has altered it. Some will destroy life through a weakness in the map that they have not been able to cope with, some will construct their lives successfully overcoming all obstructions, irritations, and adversities, others (of the dull type) may just plod along with a mediocre life. This will depend on the type of character shown within the hand. This is a major consideration as all the types – Jupiter, Saturn, Apollo, Mercury – act differently, and your summary will depend on this. You may see an excellent, successful creative left hand map yet the right hand shows dissipation of the talents. Some event has taken place to which the subject has reacted negatively, shattering hopes, goals, and happiness. This event will show up on the left hand as a break and a similar effect should show up on the Head line, Heart line, and Destiny line at the same time.

Jupiter Example
Left Hand

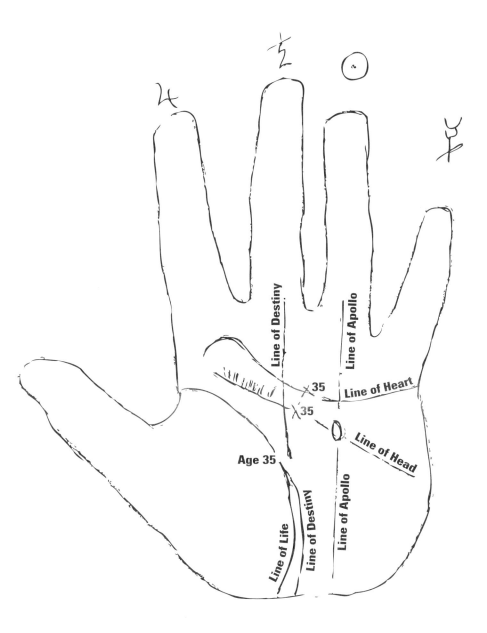

Jupiter Example
Right Hand

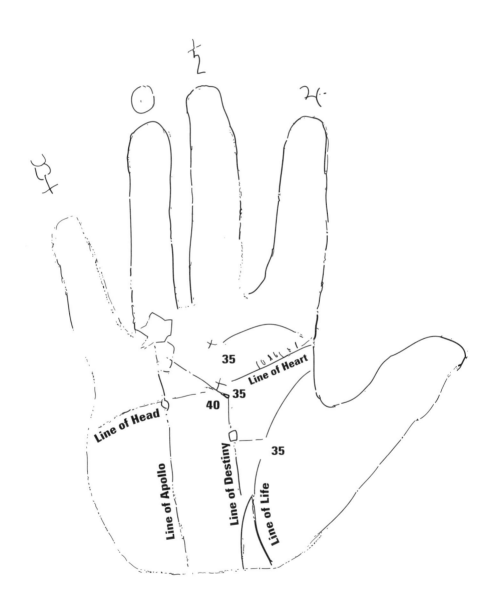

Line of Heart

35

35

40

35

Line of Head

Line of Apollo

Line of Destiny

Line of Life

Let's dream up an example here.

A Jupiterian type will be a Jupiterian all his life and act with his bigness and heartiness, pushing along wanting to be at the forefront of everything, We know that he has a great deal of pride, considering himself noble and loving, he is materially ambitious and wishes to be recognized as a powerful person. He has the same ambitions for his wife, whom he dearly loves, demanding that she too becomes "somebody." When she finally has an affair and takes off with a more considerate person, he is heartbroken and his pride takes a great shock. He turns to his weakness of drink and overeating, causing his own loss of career and finally ending in illness.

On the left hand, on the Life line, a break would show – let's say at the age of 35. This would point to a disappointment in his love life. Looking at his Heart line that runs right across the palm from side to side this indicates an excess of affection and a rather jealous nature. A break in the Heart line should show up also at the age of 35 when this major event took place. Noting also that the Heart line droops down towards the Head line, we can see that there was very little love and affection from his parents, so he experienced unhappiness in the early part of his life. With the fine lines rising from the Head line to the Heart line, he has been influenced by his parents about affairs of the heart and the lines being crossed show the trouble he is experiencing in his 35th year. Further backup of the parents influence is shown by the Destiny line being tied to the Life line and a break in the Destiny line further up the palm around the 35th year shows his misfortune and loss. Furthermore, the line of Sun – Apollo – has an island on it at roughly the same year showing loss of position and some scandal for as long as the island lasts (here you have to count the years between 35 and say 40 years). It eventually joins the Apollo line again.

Looking over to the right hand and noting that the Heart line has faded out, it shows that this person has been terribly affected by this event which altered his life completely. He has now become cold, heartless, and indifferent and his chained Saturn line, just visible above the now non-existent Heart line shows he has developed an utter contempt for the opposite sex. If he hadn't responded to his parent's lack of affection and carried around with him the feeling of being unwanted, his life could easily have gone in a different upward direction.

If we add some strengthening lines to this hypothetical example we can alter the whole scenario to a final positive outcome instead of him dying from apoplexy and gluttony.

Let's pretend again that this Jupiterian finally comes to his senses at the age of 40 and realizes what he is doing to himself. The island on Apollo had joined up also at the age of 40. The thin uneven line that developed on the Life line at the age of 35 when the unfortunate event took place indicating a temporary drifting of mind and feelings now shows a split that carries the life current onto a new course. The line runs into the Fate – Destiny – line that holds a protective square where a new opportunity comes from an older Saturn person. The line splits again, forming a trident between the Saturn and Apollo lines. And at the end of the Apollo line is a star. Here, in his new environment he will be able to put his brilliance to work in a totally new direction repairing his whole life.

Any branch line that splits off the Life line and points upwards towards the fingers or mounts is called an achievement line resulting from some event or situation that gives the subject the opportunity to try hard to achieve something and make a difference in his/her life. With Jupiterian, it is personal ambition, pride and self-worth. With the Saturnian, it will mean taking on extra responsibility, perhaps a new job or the purchasing of real estate. With the Apollonian, some form of creative effort, and with the Mercurian, it will be business involving science or health.

Now you can see with these little scenarios how the major lines and their defects come together at a point in time and life reinforcing each other. The same is true when success is shown, a step up in life, fame and wealth arrive and any other delight and sense of achievement.

If you want to get into the depths of delineation of palmistry you could make a separate diagram of both hands, put in the lines and divide them into time. Now think up a scenario for yourself and put in the defects and the strengtheners where you think they should go. Put them in pencil so you can eradicate them if they are not right. Now consider how each one of the types is going to react to the ups and downs you have drawn on the lines written on the diagrams. Write out each one separately from Jupiter to Mercury and when you compare them you will be amazed at how much insight you have gained with this absorbing exercise.

Before we get into the next chapter of the different marks on the hand, we will investigate the formation lines on the major lines of the hand that forecast shadows and lights of the life pattern.

A few more lines formed on the major lines have varying indications – see Figure 8 of line formations.

Tassels

at the end of the Life line usually indicate a weakening of the constitution, frequently with the onset of old age. When the tassels end on the line of Head there is a weakening of mental clarity – perhaps senility combined with old age. If the line of Heart is tasseled, either an emotional trauma has taken place leaving the person in an unstable condition, or the heart itself is deteriorating. Tassels at the end of the Head line indicate a person who tends to be muddled and confused.

Drooping lines

from any large line invariably indicate a disappointment of some sort. From the Heart line an event in life causes the individual to become too emotionally involved. From the line of Head – a disillusionment, a destruction of one's ideals, an obstruction where things or the life pattern need rethinking.

Upward lines

point to improving circumstances, happiness, the coming together of goals. What they are depends on where the line sprouts from and which mount it finishes on. It maybe a previous inspiration that had been put on a "back burner" and has now come to life for accomplishment.

Double or Sister lines

are very supportive of the line they run beside. For instance the line of Mars along side the line of Life strengthens the constitution and any weakness shown there. Apollo is a sister line to the Destiny line adding fulfillment to the career. Sister lines frequently protect (somewhat like the square) and heal lines that are broken, frayed or wavy.

Broken lines

are serious defects indicating danger of some sort. Some repair is necessary from some other marking, perhaps a sister line or if the broken ends overlap each other, they will carry out the repair. If a sister line is not close by, look for a square. If there are no means of repair it indicates disaster.

Dots

on the line invariably point to a patch of illness. These come and go as we all have illnesses at some time or another. They often show up on the hands of children after they have had one of the childish ailments such as measles, whooping cough, fevers, etc. After a heart attack, it may appear under the mount of Apollo close to the Heart line. Intestinal disorders would show a dot on the line of Mercury.

Chained lines

are where a number of links join together looking like a chain. Up through the line completely it points to a load of obstructions continually throughout life. Along the Head line the person is lacking in self control, is vacillating, has frequent headaches, and possibly some brain disturbance. These indispositions will only take place where the chained condition is on the time line indicating the age the subject will suffer and the period of time. Usually, the line can be repaired by a sister line. At the time a chained line is in operation, the subject will suffer from confusion and lack of self esteem. Chaining on the Life line denotes poor health at the time the chain starts to the time it finishes. With the Destiny line – who is holding the person back (or yourself) from attaining the personal goals? In other words being chained down for a specific period by other people or by surrounding circumstances. Other lines leading into each other will give the clues and answers.

Wavy undulating lines

suggest being influenced in various directions by the mount or line where the wave dips or rises. For instance a wavy line of Head would point to a lack of perseverance. On the Heart line an inconstancy regarding the affections. Always the length and position of the defect will tell you at what age it will start and finish.

We should look now in the next chapter at the marks on the lines in the hands that show the type of events to look out for.

Figure 8:
Line Formations

Ascending & Descending Lines

Capillary Lines

Sister Lines

Tasseled Lines

Square on a Line

Wavy Lines

Forked Lines

Spots on a Line

Island on a Line

Broken Lines

Chained Line

Marks to Look For

The marks we are going to look at now are different from the line formations of the previous chapter. These marks go along with the events of life, some pointing to a lucky streak or expansive period; others indicate a restriction, perhaps a destruction in some area of life depending on what and where the mark is. They add a great deal of interest to the interpretation, the triangle being the best indication of luck and success, the cross is deemed unlucky except for the Mystic Cross. This lies between the Head line and Heart line and I'll talk about that in chapter thirteen. Squares are good, grilles are bad, stars go both ways. Then we have the island, the circle, the trident, and the spearhead. Here are the details on both the lines and the mounts.

The Triangle

usually gives a feeling of pleasure and happiness no matter where it is found. It is indicative of talent and great mental qualities. If the triangle is well formed, quite clear and not composed of intersecting lines then success is assured through the mount or line on which it is situated. If the line forms an edge of the triangle the person would be well balanced but would not reach the pinnacle of success that a free and clear triangle would bring.

If you find a triangle on the Life line, here is an eloquent speaker – perhaps in politics, a speaker in the House, who possesses a certain glibness. On the Head line, there is an unusual perceptiveness within this person – they can never be fooled. On the Heart line, it points to a brilliant, cooperative and happy marriage, and on the Saturn, Apollo, or Mercury lines, great achievement is assured in the choice of life.

If the triangle is on the mount of Jupiter, this person is the diplomat; again, it might be in the employ of government with a high position, particularly if there is a line from the mount of Luna stretching across the palm to the Jupiter mount.

This would indicate service in a variety of foreign countries.

The triangle on Saturn's mount, scholarly attributes would come to the fore. Saturnian's are especially fond of delving into occult subjects or becoming involved in things of a mystical nature from which they could become well known if their knowledge is made public. Saturn loves to reach into the depths of any subject including things buried beneath the earth. These particular talents could bring both fame and fortune.

When the mount of Apollo holds a triangle, it obviously points to success in the area of artistic ability. This could be anything from a talented hairdresser, chef, architect, designer of buildings, cars, airplanes, to a writer, dancer, artist – just think of all the artistic things that go on in the world.

On the Mercury mount the triangle indicates a check on the restless qualities of the individual and turns the mind onto the executive qualities of business and money making. It also counteracts any other unfavorable signs close by. With the mount of the Moon comes a rare imaginative talent combined with scientific achievement.

The triangle on the mount of Venus gives restraint and control over the emotional self instead of rushing madly and blindly into love affairs. Taking time over choosing the right mate leads to a successful marriage and partnership. Finally, the triangle on the mount of Mars gives a presence of mind when involved in danger or a crisis is looming, particularly in warfare. Honors, medals, or a commendation could be awarded because of bravery.

The Cross

seen anywhere, tells you to be prepared for trouble. Disappointment and danger are indicated wherever it is located and it seems to force a change in life by the trouble it brings. There is one exception of a positive nature. When it is found on the mount of Jupiter, a special kind of love enters into the individual's life at a certain time shown on the Destiny (Fate) line when a line from the mount of the

Moon reaches the Destiny line. Despite any amount of struggles and aggravations encountered during the life, married life will be very happy and harmonious. But if there are little cross lines interfering with the positive flow the person may become domineering and egotistical.

When the cross shows up on the mount of Saturn, this person will have a fatalistic and morbid approach to life carrying a negative aura around which inhibits other people. When the cross on Saturn touches the Destiny (Fate) line, it points to danger from a violent death by accident, and the time on the line will point to the time when it is likely to happen.

A cross on the Apollo mount shows great disappointment while chasing after money or fame in the artistic arena. There may not be enough creativity in this person and some other area of life or occupation should be considered. The Mercury cross points out a dishonest nature. Beware of this person who is extremely deceptive, likely a con person, and he or she will be a very good liar.

The Moon cross exaggerates the talents and abilities, Venus is foolish about love and experiences many disappointments and the upper Mars mount cross carries all the indications of danger and much opposition from enemies. In some cases, there could be violence and even death from quarrels.

A cross on the Head line says a wound or accident to the Head at the time it points to. On the Life line, illness or some danger at the time indicated on the line. The Destiny line reverses the finances over a business complication, and on the Heart line there could well be the death of a loved one bringing heartfelt pain.

The Square

is always a protective device, a welcome sign on a line or mount. It is not going to protect completely but it does take the edge off any nastiness portrayed.

When the square is well formed or becomes a rectangle and the Destiny line runs through it, the time indicated on that line will show when a crisis is due or about to happen. This is usually connected to some financial loss or disaster. If the line breaks in the middle of the square, it will protect from serious loss, and if the line goes right the way through the square, the crisis will be avoided. If the square is just outside the line and just touching it and being situated under the mount of Saturn, there is protection from accidents and death – again at the time indicated on the line. There is also some protection from urinary disease, hernia, teeth, and kidney problems.

If the Head line runs through a good size square it gives extra strength to the physical body and preserves and protects the brain from over work, stress, and anxieties. When the square is above the Head line and under Saturn, the head will be protected from some sort of danger.

The Heart line of course is involved with feelings of love, passions, and emotions. Running through a square, it brings a load of trouble and upsets. If the square is directly under Saturn some disastrous or fatal event is likely to affect the lover or somebody very close.

The Life line passing through a square, even if it is broken at that time on the line, there will be a protection from death.

A square on the mount of Venus protects from unhappiness, and just inside the Life line, it gives protection from accidents or illness and hospitalization. However, when the square is on the upper edge of Venus and touching the mount of Mars it indicates detention, incarceration, imprisonment or some sort of seclusion from the world.

A square on the mount of the Moon protects on long journeys and travel of any sort, also from drowning. On the Mercury mount it restrains the restlessness and steadies the mind encouraging good writing ability, improving the person's image. On the Jupiter mount, it curtails over ambition and protects the throat from related diseases or poisons. It also gives benefit from in-laws. On the mount of Apollo, although it improves the eyesight, there seems to be a weakness regarding the purpose of the subject especially in an artistic sense. If there are also little cross lines, vanity brings folly and downfall.

The Grille

is usually seen on the mounts under the fingers indicating obstacles to be overcome that have been brought about by the uncontrolled tendencies of the person. If you look at the shape of the grille, you will see all the little openings allowing the constructive energies to escape relating to the mount on which it is situated. It is a destructive force, sapping the qualities of the mount. If there are grilles found throughout the hand, the individual's energies will be constantly drained by irritations, annoyances, and troubles, even by imagined slights.

Found on the mount of Jupiter, there is overweening pride, a very big ego, and a tendency to desire control over other people. On the mount of Saturn the grille tends to make this person morbid and melancholy. The nature is troublesome, misfortune seems to follow the person around and he/she is moody and indifferent.

On the Apollo mount, there is the desire for celebrity status that will never be attained and it will be difficult to even reach any desired success in life.

The draining of the energies of the Mercury mount leaves an unstable character who has few principles, also employing deceit and dishonesty. There is likely to be illness or health problems.

On the mount of the Moon there is restlessness, a great discontent, and a lack of mental concentration. The grille on the mount of Venus indicates excessive indulgence in pleasures and sudden changes and fancies in love affairs.

The Star

carries some importance wherever it appears on the hand and it has two meanings – positive and negative. Certainly caution is required in the area where the star is found.

Found on the Jupiter mount, honors, power, success, wealth – all comes through personal achievement. If the Destiny, Head, and Apollo lines are strong, the pinnacle of success and fame is guaranteed.

The drawback to a star being on the Apollo mount that gives great fame is the loss of one's privacy. In front of the public, the public owns the star! This lack of privacy can cause much unhappiness, especially if the media digs into the personal background.

A star on the mount of Saturn brings success and distinction but only after overcoming a mountain of problems. Yet this distinction carries some sort of unwanted, unpleasant climax – like reaching the top of the corporate ladder of brilliance but suddenly falling to the bottom. If the star is red, expect a dramatic and doomed life.

The star on the mount of Mercury marks brilliance in the area of science or business. A most expressive speaker and somehow that leads to the association of and friendship with distinguished people.

On the mount of Mars that lies just under Mercury, if the person can use patience, honors of some description will be gained. With the other Mars mount just under Jupiter, celebrity status is shown or great distinction through a martial life – perhaps engaged in a war, bravery takes place that brings the honor.

A star on the mount of the Moon brings celebrity status through the Moon's great imaginative powers. Note that if the Head line dips down onto this star, there is poor decision making and a decided mental imbalance – possibly insanity or suicide depending on other factors in the hand.

The Venus mount holding a star augers well for wonderful love affairs, eventually finding one's true love or soul mate.

If you see a star at the end of the Life line, it points to some great shock to the system and a personal injury and a star on the Heart line indicates some kind of emotional setback affecting the current of the life pattern.

Islands

are always a negative sign indicating periods of stress, weakness, or some kind of breakdown. It is a disturber, an impediment, dividing the flow of energy. Always look at the time indicated on the particular line it is on.

On the Heart line it points to heart trouble – this is probably hereditary if the island is in the middle of the line. On the Life line there will be constant indispositions from violent headaches and an illness will be shown at the appointed time.

An island on the Fate line shows heavy financial losses and misfortune at a certain period in life. On the Apollo line, scandal brings loss of name and position. On the Mercury line, the island suggests a serious illness at that point in time.

A line to the mount of Venus that holds an island says uncontrolled passion will bring trouble and disgrace to the partner. If the line forming the island on Venus runs across the hand to the marriage lines an unpleasant happening at the juncture (time of an event) will bring disgrace to the marriage.

An island on any mount violates the qualities of that mount.

On Jupiter the ambition is weakened and pride of self diminishes. On Saturn – just straight misfortune. On Apollo, creative talent is weakened by some event and Mercury's changeability and restlessness ruins any success in business, science or writing.

On the mount of the Moon there is lack of imagination and mental dullness and on the Venus mount it points to being easily led into promiscuity, passions being uncontrolled.

Circles

Luckily these are very rare marks as they are far from favorable most of the time. They seem to delight in bringing upsets, difficulties, and restrictions to the unfortunate holder of a circle. The only place where it seems to be fortunate is on the mount of Apollo where it aids success. On the other mounts it portends misfortune one way or another concerning the mount it is on. The most unfortunate one is the mount of the Moon that warns of danger of drowning.

When a circle is on any major line, check the time line. At that stage in life any misfortune that falls on the person will make him/her feel that they are literally caught up in a circle, going round and round and there seems to be no way out. Measure the circle on the line – you'll have to guess the time it takes to clear then the line can pick up again giving freedom of movement.

The circle is not usually completely round, but if it becomes a perfect round under Apollo watch out for eye trouble.

Spots/Dots

I have mentioned the dots in the previous chapter; here's a little more information. A spot or dot is usually a sign of a temporary illness. When it is a red-colored spot on the Head line, this indicates an injury, a blow or a fall to the head, producing a shock at the same time.

A bright red spot on the health line (Mercury line) means a fever and on the Life line there will be an illness with a fever – like scarlet fever. If there is a black dot on the Life line this indicates a dangerous wound, and if the upper mount of Mars is involved with a dot, this could mean receiving wounds in a fight.

A blue or a black spot, wherever it may fall, points to a nervous illness, Any of these illnesses are a temporary stop to progress in life.

The Trident and Spearhead

are the most propitious markings wherever they may be found on the hand. Both of them point to wealth and fame. They are a symbol of power and a period of unanticipated good luck. Should one or the other fall on the career (Fate) line, at the time indicated on the time

line there will be a promotion
or an unexpected windfall.
A trident on the mount
of Apollo says no matter
what financial problems this
person has, he/she will always
land on their feet.

There are three other interesting features that can be found on a hand. The
ring of Saturn, the ring of Apollo and the ring of Solomon, this last I shall talk
about in the final chapter as this is an occult feature.

The Ring of Saturn

is rather an unhappy mark to
have. Look under the Saturn
finger and you may see a half
circle starting from the finger
of Jupiter, crossing the mount
of Saturn and ending between
the Saturn and Apollo fingers.
Sometimes this semi circle is
complete, other times there
are lines across the circle and
the Saturn mount.

In a similar fashion to the Girdle of Venus, this Saturn ring also forms a barrier
against the flow of the energy current making the mount defective. No matter how
hard these people work, they achieve far less than their ambitions They have big
ideas and plans but their total lack of concentration ruins their careers, especially
if there is a dot, a cross or a star on the Fate line. A solid unbroken circle indicates
a lack of purpose and continuity of direction. Changing from one thing to another,
giving up halfway, they bring on their own failures time after time.

If there is a ring of Saturn and the Head line droops down low onto the mount
of the Moon and this is large or grilled, this restless, flighty, and changeable person
will not make much of life – only constant failures. All the prudence, wisdom, and
seriousness of the line and mount of Saturn is no longer usable – it's been cut off
by the barrier.

With a broken line on the circle there is an outlet for the energy – see if
there is a strong Will phalange on the thumb and a good Head line which will

help enormously. Without these, the ring warns of great danger, and if the ring is composed of two lines forming a cross on the Moon mount there is a definite danger of suicide.

The characteristics of the Apollo line and finger include art, music, fame, harmony, beauty, aesthetics, anything of a pleasing nature.

> With the **Ring of Apollo** found under the Apollo finger, starting from Saturn and ending on Mercury, once again this ring suggests a barrier against the free flow of this energy pattern. It is a temporary blockage where happiness takes a negative turn about. There is a deep disappointment in a relationship that seemed to be so right and going so well. At the same time, the reaction to the relationship brings a lack of interest in a creative hobby or some art form attached to the Apollo line causing a set back to career. If the ring is set below the middle (Saturn) finger, it loses some of its power and circumstances get in the way of the full development of the Apollo characteristics.

Now let's talk about money and other interesting things in the next chapter.

Figure 9:
Marks

3 Star Shapes

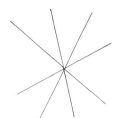

The Spot or Dot

3 Circle Shapes

3 Island Shapes

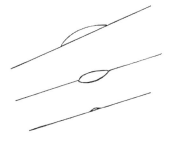

Cross Shapes & Lengths

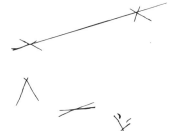

continued on next page

3 Triangle Shapes

Trident (left) Spearhead (right)

3 Grille Shapes

3 Square Shapes

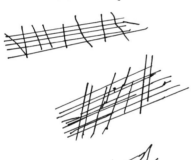

Money,
Success,
Health
and
Careers

Chapter 10

Money

Money seems to be at the forefront of most people's minds; will it be easy to come by, will you have to slog for it, win it, or are you born into it? Let's take a look at where the money is – or isn't!

Looking at hands to see where the money is, there are two things to bear in mind. First, the shape of the hands – this will tell you what type the person is (we covered this in Chapter Three). Secondly, the ambitions, goals, and motivation towards having money.

Some people are so materialistic and obsessed with money they will put everything and everybody aside to obtain it, ruining marriages, friendships, and relationships altogether. Another way to get money is to steal it. In fact, if you look at the bottom of the palm, just above the rascettes you will find the mount of Neptune. Now look at the percussion – the outer side of the palm just above the upper mount of Mars and below the Jupiter mount and you will find the mount of Uranus. These mounts, along with the mount of Pluto are recent additions to the art of palmistry, added a few years ago, opening up further information of the inner psychology of self. It is said that when a line from the Neptune mount meets the Uranus mount, a person who is desperate or greedy for money would commit murder to obtain it. An interesting feature in the palm to watch for to corroborate this statement.

As for the types, the square palm, short fingered person – the practical earth type is materially motivated, with a healthy ambition to succeed in whatever career choice is made and with an eye to making money. Productive, there is an integrity of purpose in the realm of physical effort, plodding along, and if the Will phalange of the thumb is strong they will accumulate their wealth.

The intuitive Conic hand – the fire type with the long palm and short fingers – is not inclined to plod along in search of wealth. Whatever money they have, they are inclined to give it away when their sympathies are aroused by stories of hardship. This hand is not sufficiently organized to chase after money like the Square or the Spatulate hand but they are intuitive enough to be able to speculate or get involved in a particular enterprise that brings them money. Their intuition rarely lets them down. Once they have the money they give it away!

The Spatulate hand also of the fire element, we know is the millionaire type as they have the brain and the individualists talent to develop or invent whatever the public needs to improve their lives – like the computer. It also puts a vast amount of money in their pockets.

The Philosophical hand of the element air rely on research and their great staying power to lead them to wealth. The knowledge they have and their logical thinking plus their unorthodox and sometimes eccentricity can bring money to them when their knowledge is exposed to the public. Actually, this philosophical type has less interest in money than other hands, philosophy and knowledge being their main concern, but they won't turn it down if it happens to come their way. If there is a knot on the Jupiter finger, more attention will be directed towards earning or gaining money to provide a comfortable lifestyle.

The Psychic hand belongs to the water element of lofty ideals and great imagination. Because of the sensitivity of this type, their surroundings must be pleasant, beautiful, and tasteful to preserve their emotional balance. This passive water-hand person is constantly in touch with the subconscious mind producing, in some, unproductive daydreams, There is a built-in laziness to this type. Others, who have productive and strengthening lines in the hand will build their dreams into creative productive work encouraging money to come their way. Comfort and ease of living beckons sufficiently for this person to recognize the emotional and intellectual side of life; to write about it, paint it, act it in theater work, and bare the spiritual charm of the soul for others to enjoy.

Finally, the mixed hand is a total of all four elements – fire, earth, air, and water – a rolling stone type of person. This person is more the traveling sales type with the gift of the gab, the sort who could sell anything to anybody – even the Brooklyn Bridge. They can make quite a lot of money especially if they have Conic finger tips. Their good business sense and original thinking will appeal to the masses through their innovative advertising ability.

Lines and marks in the hand will undoubtedly change these basic paragraphs altering the motivation towards the material benefits of life.

Regarding personal finances, if there is a vertical line from the base of the Jupiter finger on the outside of the hand and joining up with the Head line and the Life line, this is a good sign. No matter what happens, what events take place, somehow a way will be found to obtain the necessary funds.

The other lucky pointer is the trident on the mount of Apollo. Even if the Apollo line is quite short, as long as the trident is at the end, financial disasters

will be avoided. If they do happen to occur, a comfortable way out will be found and money will be protected.

Is there one strongly marked and distinctive cross on the mount of Apollo away from all the other lines – all by itself? Here is the indication of lottery winnings or from some other games of chance. A star attached to the Apollo line is also a pointer to a major win or attainment of money.

Being born into a wealthy family is shown by a straight line along the bottom of the fingers, just above the finger mounts. It stretches from one side of the palm to the other.

If you are a "self-made" person, now wealthy, and you have a family of young children, look at their palms. They should have a straight line across the palm. The Saturn finger is important here. If it is short – then the child could easily gamble the money away at a later date – and sometimes get lucky of course. Look at your own finger of Saturn. If it is short you may also be guilty of gambling your money away, especially if your mount of Neptune (at the bottom of the palm) is puffed and obvious and the mount of the Moon is also large. Together they suggest your Moon emotions are on a runway along with Neptune's dreams of becoming even richer without further working for it. Ambition is on the wrong track and your dreams will be broken if there is a grille on the mount of Neptune.

As an aside, here I would like to mention that a lot of material misfortune is caused by uncontrolled emotions. Losing sight of the balance of the spiritual and material energies and becoming totally wrapped up in self and the physical universe for the purpose of greed and possessiveness leads to loss. Spiritual loss equals loss of material funds, illness, poverty, unemployment. Anxiety also causes errors to be made. Loss of family and/or friends can be part of the loss ending in solitude. The spiritual loss is balanced once more by the material loss. It is an interesting spiritual law to remember.

Having said that, if you want to marry money look at your partner's hand for that straight line across the palm and the length of the Saturn finger in case he/she is a wastrel.

On your own hand, if there is a star on the mount of Jupiter and it is close to the Heart line, you most certainly could marry money. A cross on the Jupiter mount close to the end of the Heart line also says marrying money is a likelihood or to somebody who comes into money at a later date then reaching a position of importance.

There are two areas that will tell you if there is to be money coming later. Look at where the Life line and Head lines join together at the beginning. See if there are any little lines inside this area. If there are, then there will be an inheritance of some kind. If one of the lines from within the Life line and Head line reaches out and joins the Fate (Destiny) line, this is probably money that's inherited. If the line joins the Apollo line instead, it's more likely to be property that's inherited. If both Fate and Apollo lines are joined by this line then both money and property will be inherited. Remember that the star attached to the Apollo line indicates a major receipt of money and this could also be from an accident.

If you want further confirmation of this inheritance, look at the base of thumb where the lines of Influence are. Now, if there is a line from there to the base of the little finger, the wealth is from the family and two lines point to property maybe more than one.

One other thing to check on in your chase for marrying money is the thumb. If it is held close to the hand your partner will be secretive and greedy. Will you be able to share in the wealth? Better to establish that point beforehand.

If you are going to work for your money, like most of us, will you be satisfied by being employed or do you wish to work for yourself and take the chance of being successful at whatever level of satisfaction will be in your eyes?

To enjoy this satisfaction and happiness you do not need to have a big company or employ many people – unless this is your desire. You may consider it to be too many hassles and a two- or three-man company would suit you very well, you think.

You may, for instance, be a very good plumber, employed, but now feeling restless, perhaps feeling "put upon," or the company has changed hands and doesn't feel the same. Time to make a change? Your intuition is telling you to move on? Should you take that chance? Look at your line of Intuition – the semi circle that runs from Mercury to the Moon. Does it merge into your Destiny line? Then go ahead. The change into your own business will be successful and if you have a star at either end of the line of Intuition, even better. You will now have great success in your life.

If you see an island on the line of Intuition, hold back before making a change. Islands always bring poor success during the time they are operative. Measure the length of time that the island takes to become a free line again, then make your move. If you ignore this indication, your company will fail through one of your employees who perhaps, slacks on the job, is unreliable, does a bad job, and is rude to the client. Something will happen. People talk, and your company will get a bad name.

If you follow the writing in your hand you will make fewer errors, be more successful within your choices, and when the setbacks come along, as they always will, you will be prepared to handle them and sail through them without too many problems.

So let us see now where success patterns are written in the hand.

Success is usually associated with money which is supposed to bring happiness. For instance, somebody who hasn't had a great deal of money throughout life has bought a lottery ticket each week and suddenly has a win of two thousand dollars. Success at last for this person and the happiness it brings enables him/her to pay off the bills. Now, if an already wealthy person was handed two thousand dollars, it would mean nothing at all – it's just a drop in the ocean. It doesn't have the happiness and euphoria of the ordinary person, neither does it carry the pattern of success that the other person felt. Once again we are looking at the attitudes towards money and success.

So where is success going to come from? Where is it written in the hand? Both the Fate (Destiny) line and the Apollo line are major indicators, and with a bit of good luck thrown in. The good luck comes from a star on the upper mounts of Jupiter, Apollo, or Mercury, at any point along the Apollo line or right at the top of the Destiny line.

The bad luck, if you like to think of luck this way, are the islands on the Apollo line. They indicate serious problems to be overcome and invariably point to a major loss of money. Dots on this line show slander or loss of name and cutting bars will cause a setback in career. The nice thing to take the sting out of these is that they only last for a specific time. The time line will show when these setbacks will occur. Having this knowledge in advance enables you to lie back on the oars until the way is clear again, then you are free to make advances in your business and career until the next setback shows up.

Look carefully at the Apollo finger and if you see a high mount on it with several vertical lines and these are crossed by one or more lines, then you have too many talents on the go that will get in the way of true success. Choices need to be made.

Investigating the Destiny line, when there are little line loops towards the Jupiter mount, success comes only through hard work and the desire to climb

the corporate ladder. With a line from the Destiny line to the Apollo line, this confirms that the person's efforts will bring about success after the age of thirty-five. If the Destiny line is too broken, giving up this climb will come too easily.

Sometimes, this Fate line runs vertically up the center of the palm to the Saturn finger, sometimes there is only a small one just above the Heart line, then again, there may not be one at all. When the Fate line is missing there is a lack of stability, many times the hands of alcoholics and drug addicts show no Fate line. When the line is faint and weak on the hand, it usually belongs to people who are unsettled and frequently change jobs. Yet, the absence of a Fate line is often found on the hands of many successful people and millionaires. They have their health, brains, ambition, and determination, depend entirely on themselves, and achieve their goals.

The Fate line can rise from anywhere on the palm and it reflects the consequences of the person's choices in life.

If it rises from low down on the Life line and is firmly tied to it then the early part of life is likely to be sacrificed to the wishes of parents or relatives. Eventually riches and success will come from personal merit, especially if the Fate line stops by crossing its own mount and heading towards the Jupiter mount. This guarantees that success will be great and satisfactory. But if there is a break on the line as it moves across to Jupiter then expect hurdles and losses to be overcome periodically. If the line starts from the wrist and it is clear and straight up to the Saturn finger, then extreme good fortune and success will be enjoyed with very few challenges. This is a person who is likely to be employed rather than being self employed. When there is a double Fate line, an excellent distinguished career is shown. This double line or fragmenting on the line also points to making the decision to change from being employed to being self-employed. The age when this will happen will be shown on the line.

When the Fate line rises from the mount of the Moon, this is considered to be one of the best. Success is brought about with the help of the opposite sex or elders of the opposite sex. This start line is often found on the hands of celebrities who have gotten their start in just this way. When this Fate line starts from the Moon mount and another from the mount of Venus and they come together on the Fate line, this person's destiny sways between imagination on the one hand and love and passion on the other. These often get in the way of a successful career.

The "Midas" touch is shown by a line from the base of the thumb up to just below the Jupiter finger then ending in a star. Money and success from business is this same line from the base of the thumb rising to just below the Saturn finger. In fact, all lines that start from the line of Life around the thumb show increased gains and success. Surprise money and "good luck" is a line from the Head below the Apollo finger running over to the Fate line.

If a line from the Life line crosses over to Mercury, success will be from either business or science if the hand is of the Square type. The Spatulate hand would suggest success in some sort of invention or discovery and the Conic hand will be successful in speculation. Of course, we should not forget the very successful "con" person who has the crooked Mercury finger and just loves the cheating game of easy money. If there is a cross on that Mercury mount, watch out for double dealing. We once knew of a female "con" with a very crooked little finger. She had a house for sale and she sold it to eleven different people, absconded with the money – and it wasn't even her house!

Health

Health is important to success and happiness; without it, there is less likelihood of attaining the money and lifestyle you would like to have. I have added the line of Health at this point as it has a direct bearing on your life pattern, your money, success, and career. If abnormal lines show up in the hand, then disease or weakness will show up regarding your health at various times in your life.

This Health line – often called the Hepatica – starts from the wrist and continues in a straight line to the just below the mount of Mercury. Sometimes it starts from the line of Life. The Life line indicates the health during various periods of life and points to the person's general physical strength. If it starts here there are usually digestive ailments.

The Health line should run straight up the hand – straighter the better. The line being completely absent shows an extremely robust and healthy constitution.

A prominent or very obvious line points to nervousness, a weak constitution, and a delicate bodily system, especially if it touches the Life line at any point. A

twisted and irregular line indicates liver and/or kidney disease plus biliousness. A great deal of care must be taken over the choice of food. When the Health line is formed of little straight pieces there will be stomach problems at various times in life also very bad and uncomfortable digestion.

Little islands – always the trouble makers – on the line is indicative of lung and chest troubles especially if the person has long filbert-shaped nails.

When the Health line is heavily marked and joins onto both the Heart and Head lines, there may well be brain fever and with little red spots the bodily system is inclined to become feverish.

A red Health line gives signs of heart disease, also apoplexy. Break or split lines show illnesses for a short period of time. If they are continuous a change of residence would be advantageous even necessary.

The time line on both the Health and Life lines will show when illness will take place. If the body is permanently weak or delicate then a career must be chosen that suits the system. Unfortunately, it may have to be a second choice.

There are many indications on the palm for money and success, they just have to be sorted out and applied to the type of hand and the character of the subject, along with the career that would be most suitable.

Careers

In our search for career fulfillment, I think many of us have tried a variety of jobs as we gradually matured. Some were lucky enough to get into jobs they really enjoyed, spotted trends within them, used their brains and determination to develop them, and made a fortune. Witness Walt Disney and his creative imagination that brings the public in to enjoy his world – the mount of Luna (Moon) influence. Bill Gates, who took the world by storm with his computers, opened up communication between people around the globe, with the Mercury mount influence. These are just two examples of people who stepped right in and found their niche.

How about the rest of us? Is your temperament suited to the job you are in? Did you meekly follow in your parents footsteps or some other member of the family directed your life where you didn't want to go?

If you look at the Fate line on the right hand and see many little lines traveling up, this would point to the number of different jobs you've attempted in your search for the right one that brings satisfaction and fulfillment.

Each of the different hand types will have a leaning towards certain types of jobs which they hope will eventually become a career.

The mounts on the hands will also bring their influence to bear on the many choices available. Because there are so many to choose from it is usually by trial and error, a sort of "hit and miss" situation most of the time. The mounts are the guidelines for zeroing in on the most suitable career choices.

There is frequently a prominent mount on the hand followed by a secondary one that is almost as strong, indicating the qualities associated with these mounts are probably the best choices for a career.

If there are more than two fairly strong mounts there are a number of different qualities that will need to be combined and balanced and you will come across a wide variety of career choices. Here is how a combination could work. You've looked your right hand and found that the Mercury, Pluto, and Moon mounts are all prominent. How do you go about combining them into a successful and satisfying career? Mercury likes to write and talk and you have that strong indication in your hand. Moon likes to travel and be on the move and Pluto – the transformer – has contempt for the atrocities and kidnappings that are taking place in various parts of the world. The combination of these qualities would/could lead to the career as an overseas journalist (Mercury and Moon) exposing the unscrupulous and vindictive behavior and violence (Pluto) in your newspaper or on television (this last if you have a line joining the Pluto and Uranus mounts). Eventually, you could put together a book (Mercury) with photographs of the atrocities (Moon) bringing the realities to the public's attention, demanding political intervention.

It just takes a little bit of thought in combining the qualities of the various mounts. Below I have put a variety of the qualities of the mounts into sections for you to choose from.

Jupiter Mount

We know that Jupiter's qualities are expansion, excess, and enthusiasm – especially for money! The interest would be as a cashier, banker, casino operator/owner, financier, a broker, or the stock exchange. Other interests

are lawyer, barrister, judge, councilor, magistrate, teacher, professor, politics, treasury minister, ambassador, diplomat, overseas embassies, doctor, physician, theologian/ordained minister, tour guide, sports and coaching, especially golf and archery.

At the lower end of the scale: a capitalist, a plutocrat, or a successful embezzler.

Saturn Mount

Saturn's qualities are regulating, conservative, self sufficient and somewhat materialistic. The career interests are along organized lines such as science involving engineering, chemistry, geology. Things of the earth appeal – coal mines, archeology, farming, excavation. Being of a structural nature, technical writing, history, economics, police force, law, a coroner, medical examiner would be of interest. Real estate, an undertaker, mortgage broker, pharmaceuticals, and politics could also apply.

At the lower end of the scale: a mercenary. Also being suppressive and malicious.

Apollo Mount

The qualities of this mount are authority, self expression, creativity, ambition. Their interest usually deals with beauty and variety, but if the Saturn mount has any influence on this mount they will be interested in biology, health, and health food stores. Other careers involve gift stores, theatre, drama teacher, art and art galleries, dancing, sculpture, pottery, a game show host, children's playgrounds and parks.

The lower end of the scale suggests being a "little dictator," arrogant and condescending, coming on with being a "bit too royal."

Mercury Mount

Mercury's qualities are communication, the mind, thinking, and travel. Thinking and acting quickly they are suited to careers in accountancy, advertising, or the travel industry, speech writer, speech therapist, elocution teacher, graphologist, journalist, mail carrier, the publishing industry, writer – novels and non fiction – a notary public, secretary, and involvement in youth clubs.

The lower tendencies are cheating, forgery and stealing.

Mars Mount

Mars qualities are action, assertion, impulse, and courage. Careers in the armed forces, police force, ambulance, or fire service. Builder, carpenter, barber, dentist, engineer, prison guard, lumberjack, sports – boxing, martial arts, fencing, football.

The other side of Mars is violence, uncontrolled anger, being a hoodlum or a burglar.

Moon Mount

The qualities of the Moon are cutting and conclusive, putting an end to uncertainty in a caring manner. In bakery, catering, delicatessen, grocery clerk, hotel, janitor, midwife/nurse, navy personnel. The Moon's creative and imaginative side offers advertising, publishing, language schools, interpreter, photographer, painter, writer of children's books, librarian.

The lower side of the Moon is miserable, always crying, emotional, too docile, clinging and fickle.

Venus Mount

Venus qualities are anything that appeals to the senses such as, love, marriage, finery, music, sweets, art. Careers with beauty are at the top of the list: beauty parlor, hairdresser, bridal shops, sweet shops, catering, restaurants, wine stores, social clubs, dance schools, dressmaker/tailor, florist, gardener, massage and aromatherapy, and singing.

Their faults are being slipshod, untidy and over eating.

Uranus Mount

Uranus qualities are invention, discovery, independence, liking to be different and going against the rules. Career as a revolutionary, humanitarian, insurgent, mutineer are exciting to them. They also like to be different by being an astrologer, clairvoyant, or metaphysician. Other interests are being a pilot, an innovative aircraft and automobile designer, radio announcer, novelist, antique dealer, a lineman, or a pioneer.

Their lower qualities are being stubborn, inflexible, meddlesome and indiscreet.

Neptune Mount

Neptune's qualities are imagery, fantasy, inspiration, idealism. Careers that most attract are parapsychology, psychic phenomena, and all the New Age stuff. Also on the career list is being an anesthetist, deep sea diver, violinist, herbalist, navy in submarines, oil industry, film industry, video stores, and drug rehabilitation centers.

Bottom of the heap of Neptune's undesirable traits are self-deception, drug/alcohol addict, counterfeiter, fraud, and charlatan.

Pluto Mount

Pluto's qualities are of the transforming kind. It destroys to make something better and to bring about change, it has a great deal of power. Careers in police work dealing with crime, also as a private investigator, a political spy, research, psychoanalysis, hypnotherapy, the construction and demolition industry, hostage negotiator. Work in a crematorium or as an embalmer.

It's lower qualities being sadistic, a criminal, a gunman or a kidnapper.

The major line to consider when you are looking for a career is the Saturn/Fate/Destiny line. This line tells you how successful you will be. When your career will be interrupted by obstacles will be shown on the time line telling you not to push against them. Take them in your stride without anxiety and being over emotional for they will pass. If the Fate line is long and unbroken, running from the wrist to the Saturn mount, there will be a successful career.

When the line stops and starts again – so will your career. This is likely to be a time of change for a career, but if the line stops suddenly at a cross you are facing difficult circumstances. If there is a star at the end of the line you are likely to reach the top of your career and gain recognition.

Looking at both the Fate line and the mounts you can select the career(s) that you feel are right for you and the Fate line will guide you with the events to come.

Love,
Romance,
Marriage

Chapter 11

What's the difference between love and romance?

**Romance** is sentiment and ideality, an infatuation, an instant desire, an element of sexual excitement. Love is supposed to be the mount of Venus, the third phalange of the thumb, but if that phalange is long and thin on the thumb, this leans more towards the passionate, romantic, and sensual side of life. If you look just inside the Life line on the Influence lines and you see a line cutting into the Heart line there will be a lot of interference in romantic affections.

If there is a line rising from just below the mount of Venus inside the mount of Mars, this is just romance not true love. One person will lose any sympathy and affection for the other. See whose hand the line is on and you will know who loses the interest. If the line fades out and renews itself further on then the romance will take off again. When it fades away once more – that's it – total separation. When this line runs down and joins a cross line and it runs right across the hand, whoever has this marking on the hand will come to hate the other person. He/she will do an injury to the other party, depending on where the line ends – on the Life, Head, Fate, or Heart line. Such is romance!

Numerous lines near the line of Life shows a person who depends on affection. Very passionate, they have plenty of affairs, some illicit and intriguing. They are always looking for love and a commitment which invariably drives the other party away. But if there is a full smooth mount of Venus, then the romance is simply enjoyed without ties to each other.

When the Heart line lies right across the palm there is an excess of affection – a bit of a smother love – and a tendency towards jealousy, especially if the lines rises to the outside of the hand by the base of the Jupiter finger. Jealousy frightens off the boy/girl friend. If the line of Heart has a crowd of little lines rising into it – whoever has it on the hand will be a flirt, inconstant, have lots of affairs on the side with no lasting affection – that's not much of a romance, nor will love be attained. With little or no Heart line, this person is not capable of feeling a deep affection; romance with these people goes nowhere.

Romance – although seeming to be genuine at the time – is merely a temporary interlude.

Love, on the other hand, is totally different. You feel comfortable with the other person, no feelings of insecurity wondering if he/she is cheating. Somehow you learn to love a little at a time. You find yourself listening inwardly to what the other has to say and noting how you are treated. Then, one day, you realize that love, in its truest sense, has finally arrived. Acceptance of the other person with all his/her faults and imperfections is the road to unconditional love; it's also a lifelong friendship that takes root and grows.

What are you seeking for in a lifelong partner? A clear Heart line indicates a person who has a love of family, can be relied on and has sympathy for others, but if the line starts high – almost at the base of the Jupiter finger, jealousy can rear its head at times.

If the line begins low on the hand and runs in a straight line, there is affection for family, but the person finds it difficult to express these feelings. The line starting between the first and second fingers brings a warmth and sensuality into the love, but starting between the second and third fingers there is a negative attitude towards love. If you really love this person you will need to be very understanding.

Just remember this guideline when investigating love in the hand. The higher the Heart line, the warmer and more affectionate the nature will be. The lower it lies, the nature is colder and more calculating.

A double Heart line has a great deal of love and affection as well as physical strength and endurance in sexual encounters.

If the Head, Heart, and Life lines are joined at the start, this person is most unreasonable in affections. This will spoil the family life bringing unhappiness and disappointment all round. If the Heart line is long and thin then revenge will be carried out when this person is frustrated. Downward branches from the Heart line that do not touch another major line will bring disappointments with your lover/partner and if that line droops down to the mount of the Moon you can expect quarrels and uncontrollable emotions from the other person.

Surprisingly, when the line of Heart rises from the Saturn line, this person will be very passionate in attachments. Saturn, being usually quite cold by nature, the Heart line seems to melt the cold heart giving Saturn a sensual and passionate ardor. When the Heart line starts with a small fork on the Jupiter mount this individual is true and honest in love and a very happy person if the line is high. If you see white spots on the Heart line of your partner you know you will be very happy in love. Will this finally lead to marriage? What does your hand and the hand of your partner say about this most important event? As lovers, what do you know and expect from each other if a further step is taken? I mentioned the four elements earlier – the Fire, Earth, Air and Water, each will have a different idea of a union.

Fire hands

as lovers are positive, confident, and willing to take the lead and make the decisions.

Earth hands

as lovers are usually straight forward and dependable in all situations.

Air hands

as lovers look for mental rapport; there will be many invigorating conversations.

Water hands

as lovers are sensitive, vulnerable, somewhat naïve. They focus on caring and being cared for, and can be easily upset if they feel they are not getting enough attention and love.

How *you* love and how you *are* loved are very import issues and these are the foundations on which your union will grow.

All in all, there are many choices to be made before the final decision of carrying on with your love affair and eventually tying the knot of Oneness. Are you really compatible and will you experience happiness or end up in separation and divorce?

The Marriage line(s) can be found on the mount of Mercury, under the little finger, starting from the outside of the hand. They are sometimes referred to as the lines of Affection or the lines of Union. They represent love affairs, marriages and the usual ups and downs, the trials and tribulations that all marriages go through. We have discussed love affairs in the previous paragraphs and a line on the marriage line itself can confirm if a marriage is contemplated. A short line close to a long line on the marriage line indicates a very deep affection and marriage may be in the offing. Only the long lines relate to marriage.

Here we must also look to the Life line and the line of Fate (Destiny) or both, for these point to a change in life and position. If you look at the marriage lines on the mount of Mercury this will give some idea of the age when a person will marry. When the marriage line is closer to the Heart line, there will be an early marriage, a teen marriage between the ages of sixteen to twenty-one. Nearer the center of the mount of Mercury marriage is likely between the ages of twenty one and twenty-eight. If the line is right over the side of the mount, marriage will be a little later, between the ages of twenty-nine and thirty-six. If the line snakes even further across to the mount of Saturn, the marriage will take place later and later.

Usually there is one line longer than the other and clearly marked. If it is closer to the little finger, marriage will take place very late in life. If this line turns upwards, there will be no marriage. If there is a cross on the mount of Mercury and a cut on the marriage line, the marriage will be called off or the engagement broken.

All these and the following indications should be qualified by the Life and/ or Fate lines. Watch for the cross, the cross line or the break on these lines then note the good or bad traits on the line of marriage. These two major lines give a fairly close date of the changes or influences.

With a long straight clear line of marriage there will be happiness and contentment and if this line continues on to the line of Apollo, a wealthy marriage is shown, particularly if a line from the Moon mount runs up and joins the Fate line. If the marriage line continues on towards the Saturn mount and cuts through it, adversity and unhappiness will be experienced.

A broken line of marriage running across to the Life line indicates divorce or separation and overlapping lines show periods of reconciliation. When this line breaks in two, there will be a sudden break to the marriage. If there are two parallel lines very close together on the marriage line a family member may intervene, try to help or influence the marriage in some way.

When there is a very obvious marriage line with fine lines dropping down towards the Heart line, the partner will develop an illness leaving him/her in bad health and when the line develops a long gradual curve the bad health will bring death.

Branches on the downside of the marriage lines show a marriage of heartbreak, on the contrary, if they are uplifting then a very happy marriage is indicated.

An island on the marriage line also points to unhappiness, and with a star at the end of the line, the marriage will end in an explosive situation due to adultery and unfaithfulness. If the line is full of islands and drooping lines, the subject would be well advised to avoid marriage at all cost, particularly if the line is drooping towards the center of the palm and there is a fork at the end. Divorce or judicial separation will take place.

Finally, when the marriage line sends a little branch towards the Apollo mount and into the Apollo line, this person will marry someone famous, well known, or holding an honorable position. But if the line turns down and cuts off the Apollo line – whoever holds this line in the hand will lose his/her position after marrying. If there is a deep line from the mount moving downwards and cutting into the marriage line, there will be many obstacles and much opposition before the marriage takes place.

Look for a fine line running parallel and almost touching the marriage line then you will know that deep affection will continue throughout married life.

Children,
Retirement,
Widower-
Widowhood

Chapter 12

Figure 10:
Retirement

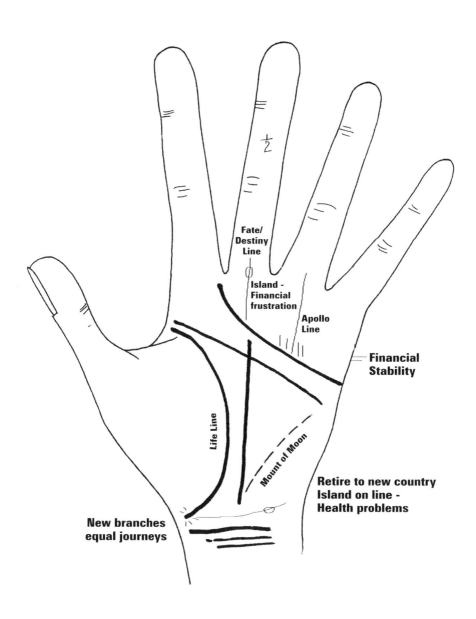

Fate/
Destiny
Line

Island -
Financial
frustration

Apollo
Line

Financial
Stability

Life Line

Mount of Moon

Retire to new country
Island on line -
Health problems

New branches
equal journeys

Children

Children, Do you want them? Do you like them? How many would you like to have? The last two questions are a bit of an enigma just as the child lines on the hand pose the same problem.

Lines relating to children can be found at the end of the marriage line on the percussion side of the hand. They are small fine vertical lines. It is said that children are promised by small cross lines on the marriage line. Straight lines for boys and slanting lines for girls. But whose children are they?

One person who is unable to conceive may have no lines on her hand at all and if she is glad about this fact then the lines will not be there at all. Recall we change our own reality by our thoughts and our thoughts and desires show up as lines and marks on the hands.

Now, another person who also cannot have children of her own has multiple lines on the child lines that says she will have a football team! What the lines are saying is that children will feature in her life some way and of course, the palmist has to figure it out – so be careful what you say or promise.

This lady who loves and desires children has grown her own lines on her hands. To satisfy her deep desire, she may be a day care worker, kindergarten teacher, a grade school teacher, a children's librarian, a nurse in a children's hospital, a care worker in an orphanage. On the other hand, she may have adopted them, or is constantly surrounded by nieces and nephews. She may have step children that her husband has brought along from his previous marriage. From these step children she will be delighted to eventually become a grandmother, So you can see how unreliable these children lines can be.

A more reliable sign of producing children or with the above example of getting children is the tiny influence lines that branch down just inside the Life line. These will show up during the child bearing years near the middle section of the Life line whether they are conceived, adopted or are just family members. These lines represent responsibilities arriving in a woman's life – they may well be children that have been conceived or being responsible for children in some other way. If there is a tiny branch showing further down, don't mistake it for a child, it is more likely to be taking on the responsibility of an older person later on in life.

A line encircling the base of the thumb is called the family ring, meaning family members. A line reaching halfway down, reaching out towards the influence line could be a child or children who make a big impact on you.

Whether they are your own children, adopted or family members, including step children, check the child lines in their hands. The lines start from the outside of the marriage lines and run in towards the hand. If the lines are clearly marked they indicate a good strong, healthy body. Check the Life line at the same time for confirmation. When the lines are faint or wavy then the health is not so good.

Look carefully for those nasty little trouble making islands. If there is one at the beginning of the line, this suggests that the child will be delicate during the early years of life. If the line is strong after the island has closed, then strength and health will follow. If the line ends at the island and there is no continuation of the line or help lines from anywhere else on the hand, then death is indicated.

There may be one child who has a longer line in the hand which is obviously strong and outstanding, it is likely that this one will be more important to you and have more impact on you than the others. Check your own hand to see if you have a matching line, perhaps your partner/husband has one and shows a particular fondness for this child. If the child lines in a male hand are clear and strong, he will have an extremely affectionate nature and a great love for children.

However many children you have, they all have their different personalities and need to be understood to bring out the best in them. The shape of the hand will give you clues as to what is hidden inside the child that needs to be encouraged and developed.

Children with square hands are of a practical nature. Easy going, slow moving, they tend to think slowly before coming to usually sound conclusions. These children are materially oriented rather than being intellectually inclined. Wherever their practical and constructive natures lead them, they should be encouraged to recognize the creative side of life and learn to appreciate art in their own way. This could lead them into the creative expression of their business like minds.

Children with spatulate hands enjoy sport of all kinds and may be inclined towards making a career in it, especially if the child has a determined and fixed nature. These children are very active, they are also artistic in most original ways and they should be encouraged to develop the areas they are most interested in. They like to work with their hands and to develop their own ideas. This is their most valuable asset and this too should be encouraged. They should be introduced to reading at an early age especially in the areas of travel, science, and the arts.

Children with the psychic – pointed – hand can be quite difficult to instruct and to understand. They are somewhat impractical as they live in their own world of fantasy and dreams. Gentle discipline is required along with getting them to understand about punctuality and tidiness both mental and physical. They are hopelessly untidy most of the time. They are drawn towards writing, music, and painting; and these creative areas must be encouraged and developed.

Children with the conic hand are not easy to get along with. They are highly intelligent but they are ruled by their emotions and are easily led by other people. Their moods change with the bat of an eyelid, so be prepared for the swings and roundabouts from their unstable natures. They are influenced by artistic things rather than being artistic themselves, unless their finger tips are square. This squareness will help to bring out their creativity. They are very clever quick thinkers and their judgement is usually correct for which you should give ample praise. These children, because of their intelligence should be introduced to and encouraged to pursue a variety of subjects. They will eventually eliminate the less attractive and follow up with the ones that have the greatest appeal.

Retirement

Retirement. Here it is at last. After all the years you've put in to working, decision making, battling the finances, handling all the frustrations of living, now you can sit back and please yourself.

The transition from public life to retirement is viewed in different ways by different people. Some see this as a loss of status and the crumbling of the structure of their lives. Others have looked forward to this time and now don't know what to do with themselves. The days are long and empty because no plans for the future have been made. The sensible ones have taken stock of themselves beforehand, viewed the things they previously have wanted to do but haven't had the time or the opportunities to do them. They have now decided where next to put their energies.

The end of your career and into retirement is a whole new journey filled with new opportunities and prospects. In fact, this can be an exciting and productive time in life. This life-altering change will bring growth in a different direction as all change should. New ideas will come to you if you open your mind to the new world around you – one you haven't had time to really take a good look at. You have time now to travel and explore new places if you are inclined in this

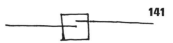

direction. You will most certainly learn something new about yourself as you will not be influenced by the people and opinions of the material world you have just stepped away from.

There are three areas of the hand that will give you information about your retirement: the Life line, the Destiny (Fate) line, and the Apollo line.

The Life line points to your physical well being, how you view your life so far and whether you will be able to accept the change from a structured daily existence to one that is empty each day until you have filled it with your desires or your next chosen assignment. The other items to consider are your family relationships. How do they feel about your choice to retire? Are they concerned about your loss of a steady income? Is your pension enough to cover your lifestyle without hardship? Do you have funds put by to fall back on to help you enjoy your new existence? Have you discussed your new interests and goals with your partner – the most important person in your life? And lastly, do you have the motivation to do what you would really like to do?

The Life line will answer some of your questions, perhaps even set you in a direction you hadn't thought of before. Look at the lower portion of your Life line, towards the base of the hand. If it is strong and obvious, this indicates you will enjoy a far better, less stressful life, one where you can reach any goal you set for yourself. You will also have time to pursue the old ones along with new ideas that will crop up. These will bring great satisfaction and improved health.

If there are a number of new branches shooting out from this area of the Life line, it suggests journeys and visits to different places. Does the bottom of the line split into two with one end pointing to the mount of the Moon? Perhaps you will decide to leave your place of birth and finally retire to a country that you've always fancied, somewhere warm with beach and water? However, if you see an island there, it shows symptoms of health problems or a number of frustrations for the length of time the island is in operation.

I mentioned family reactions to your retirement because the Life line shows events concerning members of the family, plus your own inner hidden conflicts that you will have to face in the course of disagreements about what you want to do with your retirement time. Any problem with finding something useful and constructive to do or any problem with your spouse could lead you off the track you wish to take. Many times a married couple become closer together, but if there are disagreements and your spouse has a sense of insecurity and the structure of the routine seems to be falling apart, this can cause a great deal of stress leading perhaps to sexual frustration. In turn, this frustration can lead to ignoring family and becoming totally involved in accumulating money.

This sometimes happens to business men and women, and if a ring suddenly appears on the little finger you will know he/she is engrossed in money and the material side of life instead of love, enjoyment, and togetherness. Another indication of being wrapped up in the financial world is the wearing of a heavy ring on the Jupiter finger.

Look now towards the Apollo line as this indicates a successful retirement. It is usually a short line beginning just above the Heart line and running up into the Apollo finger. This shows your ability to adapt to the new challenges of retirement, also from a feeling of satisfaction with the years of service you've previously put in. Apollo is your personal fulfillment – your pride in yourself for what you have accomplished. The stronger that little Apollo line is above the Heart line the more contentment you will get from your retirement time.

If you see a set of parallel lines just above the Heart line you have financial stability, this you should point out to your spouse to allay any fears. The more of these lines you have then the more money will be available.

Making the move from a public to a private life is shown on the Fate line. It shows when changes will take place that alter the structure of our lives. Retirement covers many aspects of life – health, finances from the two previous lines we have discussed, plus travel, new growth, and new interests.

The upper part of the Fate line is the one you should take into consideration. It is just above the Heart line moving up into the Saturn finger. A break in that line with a continuation shows early retirement might take place providing there is a money fund to fall back on. If the Fate line branches off at retirement time or there are many little branches, this points to an interest in many things and you will have to put them in priority order.

An island at the end of the Fate line brings frustrations in the financial area. During the time the island is in operation there will more than likely be a shortage of income or funds. If you have a strong inner adaptability you will weather the storm of this Destiny line.

Hand shapes give an indication of the type of retirement you would prefer.

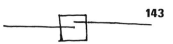

Earth

Earth hands, the square palms with the short fingers don't care much for change. They find retirement difficult, preferring to work as long as possible. Even if they own their own company they'll likely keep going till death takes them away from it. If they could get themselves to retire, they would enjoy being out amongst nature and being in the bush. Photography, art, carpentry, and outdoor jobs would give them a feeling of accomplishment and enjoyment in their retirement years.

Air

Air hands, the square hands with long fingers get involved in all sorts of activities. They have a low boredom threshold needing constant intellectual stimulus. They join travel clubs, enjoy flying – even taking flying lessons – study groups feed their intellect. They are good at talking and writing, they like to share their knowledge. These are the teaching people whether they get paid for it or not. Do you have a square under the index finger? Then you are one of the folks who love to teach. Writing a book is another interest and retirement is the time to do it.

Fire

Fire hands with the oblong palm and short fingers join clubs and get involved with community projects. Active and outgoing, they love to be in charge of people and like to arrange activities of all kinds to keep people interested in life. Some who are over active should be very careful of injuries and accidents.

Water

Water hands with the rectangular palm and long fingers enjoy retirement and look forward to it. Being of a lazy nature they like to lay around, reading, watching TV. They also enjoy boating, sailing, cruises, going to fashion and beauty shows, and getting involved in amateur theatricals. Some who are mentally active get down to writing poetry, composing music, learning to play an instrument – often the violin – or just sitting back to enjoy it.

If you are the traveling kind, do consult the travel lines in the hand. They can be found on the mount of the Moon just on the edge of the palm opposite the mount of Venus. If there are many lines there will be many trips and vacations here and there, such a restlessness there is here. If they start at the percussion side, the choice of transport will be by sea and air. If the lines are actually on the Moon mount, the choice will be mainly by land – car, train, bus.

If the travel line ends in a cross there will be a disappointment with the journey and vacation. A square on the travel line points to danger, but the traveler will be protected. An island on the line predicts loss and a star on the travel line implies great danger. Always consult the travel lines before starting out.

Widower-Widowhood

Widowhood. All good things must eventually come to an end and the death of a beloved partner is the saddest of all. Knowing ahead of time which of you is going to pass on first takes some of the pain away. Once again, we are looking at changes that alter the structure of your total existence and this advance knowledge will give you time to make plans and mentally arrange your future.

There are many indications within the hand foretelling of the eventual separation of a life-long partnership. We will start by looking closely at the Life line and gradually integrate the other directions that point to death.

If the Life line is made up of little chains, this shows bad health. If the line is broken on the left hand, this points to a dangerous illness and when the right hand also breaks, it signifies death is about to take place. This will be confirmed when a branch line bends towards the mount of Venus.

The line of Influence near the Life line can also be an indicator. When it starts to fade it shows the beginning of the separation. When it vanishes altogether, it usually means death and the end of the companionship. The line of Health is another vital pointer to death taking place eventually when it joins up to the Life line. More than likely from a disease that has already been indicated previously in the Health line. No matter how long the Life line is, the meeting point of the Health and Life lines will be the point of death and this could take place anywhere along the Life line.

The Head line when it is abnormally short foreshadows an early death from some sort of mental problem and if the line is broken under the mount of Saturn there could be a sudden early death from some disaster.

Looking now at the line of Marriage on the mount of Mercury, when it drops down or curves towards the Heart line then the partner will die first. With fine hair lines dropping from the marriage line to the Heart line, it foretells of a great deal of trouble with the bad health and illness of the partner.

A black dot on the marriage line points to eventual widowhood. A break in the line foretells of the sudden death of the partner, and if the line ends in a star on the mount of Mercury it confirms the death of the partner. Another indicator is when the marriage line is cut at its end by another line, then the partner will go first.

Sudden death of the partner is indicated by a line drooping to the Head line that contains a small cross on the curve. If this curve is long and gradual without the cross then ill health will cause the death.

I have mentioned the cross in the chapter on Marks to Look For. This is one of the indicators of a change of lifestyle that death invariably brings. Trouble usually accompanies the cross. When there is one on the mount of Saturn and it touches the Fate line there is a danger of a violent death by accident and if it is over the Heart line it confirms the death of a loved one.

Sad and heart breaking it is for some, for others it represents freedom they have been waiting for, the information of this event is there in the palm of the hand. Studying the line of Influence again, you will be able to see what help and guidance you will receive from other family members to help you over this tragic time.

Are You Psychic, Spiritual, A Mystical Person?

Chapter 13

Figure 11:
Are You Psychic?

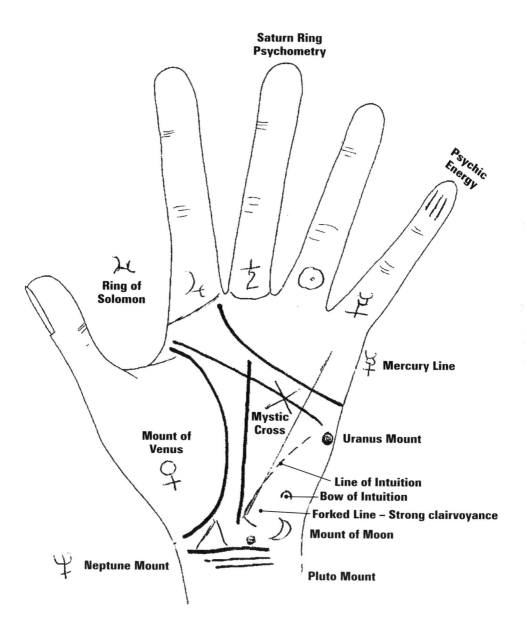

Saturn Ring
Psychometry

Psychic Energy

Ring of
Solomon

Mercury Line

Mystic
Cross

Uranus Mount

Mount of
Venus

Line of Intuition

Bow of Intuition

Forked Line – Strong clairvoyance

Mount of Moon

Neptune Mount

Pluto Mount

Are You Psychic?

Everybody is born with psychic ability. Watch small children playing with their unseen friends. They can see them, talk to them, and hear what they are saying. Adults usually scoff at them saying it is just imagination, unless their own psychic ability has developed into free flow. How can you tell? Do you have feelings or impressions of when things are right or wrong? Do you follow these hunches or just dismiss them as something quirky? On the other hand, if you use them and let them guide you towards your purpose in life then you are genuinely intuitive and psychic.

The palms of your hand show this ability and once again there are a number of indications pointing to this wonderful energy pattern that flows through you.

The little finger of Mercury shows psychic communication and sensitivity to the spiritual realms. Look at the tip of the finger and you may see a number of vertical lines. The deeper, longer and clearer they are, then your psychic energy flow is very subtle and powerful. This energy is used in both a material and spiritual sense, activating all seven Chakra energy points at different times depending on the circumstances of the day.

"Listening" to (clairaudience or telepathy) inner communication or just following your intuition can guide you to a meaningful future to develop your potential, your skills, talents, and abilities, also making you aware of your own limitations. This valuable stream of energy will help you remove physical, mental, and spiritual blocks guiding your life path towards happiness and fulfillment.

There are three phalanges on the finger. The top portion uses subtle psychic abstract energy whereby you can zone in during your meditation time to fulfill your spiritual needs and develop an expressiveness in speech that causes people to regard you as an impressive person.

The middle phalange puts to use the guidance of diplomacy that you absorbed from your meditation, enabling you to negotiate diplomatically and fairly with all people. Horizontal lines across the vertical lines tell you that at times you will run into conflict with stubborn people.

The third and lower phalange – the material realm, shows how you accept and participate in the physical matters of intimacy, physical pleasure, and sexuality – all an important part of the life and energy balance.

If you don't have vertical lines on the phalanges and you know you are intuitive and psychic – don't despair. They don't show up on every hand as there are many other pointers to these abilities.

Continuing on with the Mercury line, if there is a fork on it and one fork points to the mount of the Moon, there is an unusual perceptiveness, even a strong clairvoyance. In this case it is important to trust yourself in what you

"see" and also to "listen" to your inner voice. If you have this wonderful ability and don't use it, you may find negative influences impinging on you causing difficult relationships with people or communication with them is blocked.

Another area of the palm to search for these faculties is for a strong line of Intuition. This suggests you should always act on your hunches and feelings for they will always be correct. If there are two lines close together, pay attention to your dreams, try to remember and record them for they are "true" and invaluable.

The line of Intuition reaching to the Head line indicates a very good psychic or spiritual teacher. If the line reaches the Destiny line your psychic abilities will ultimately take you on a long rewarding journey. Here is the ability for telepathy, clairvoyance, foreseeing the future, but all these gifts must be developed or they will remain dormant and benefit no one, including yourself.

One further thing here is the Cross of Intuition – sometimes called the Bow of Intuition. This is a semi-circular mark that lies in the area of the Moon mount. Strong intuition and psychic ability lies here and this is invariably found on the hands of mediums, channelers, psychics and people who have the outstanding ESP faculty.

Are You Spiritual?

People with the psychic (idealistic) hand are frequently the ones of a spiritual nature. They somehow feel the underlying awe and mystery of life within their being. Both the magic of the universe and its inexplicable phenomena have a huge appeal for them. Their intuitive faculties are highly developed and they are alive to feelings and impressions and they rely on their instincts. They have a genuine interest in mankind.

Spiritual inclinations can be found in the center of the quadrangle between the lines of Heart and Head. In there is what is known as the Mystic Cross. It indicates a person who is skilled in the metaphysical world and perhaps in the use of manipulating the energies of the universe. It is also a sign of the ability to personally expand spiritually with a definite sense of purpose.

The Mystic Cross right in the center of the quadrangle gives a strong psychic sense and a large amount of crosses on the hand puts the psychic ability to use.

If the Mystic Cross is found at the end of the quadrangle on or near the mount of Jupiter, the person with this symbol is purported to possess a great amount of spiritual energy, occultism know-how, plus a measure of superstition, but this energy will be used specifically for their own gain and bolster their sense of importance. If the Cross is further away from Jupiter then the application of these abilities will be implemented towards humanity.

Saturn has a strong interest in the development of spiritual things. Along with the Mystic Cross, the Saturn mount may have a ring encircling its base adding to the desire of the search for hidden powers. A good ring around the base suggests the power of psychometry – being able to foretell the future and the past by holding an object belonging to another person. The Saturn ring most definitely has magical and occult powers, plus the love of psychic exploration. If there happens to be a triangle on the mount of Saturn as well then these powers are twice as powerful. These powers can be used to make a living. A long upper phalange on the Saturn finger increases the psychic perception. Perception being a very creative medium it will only yield results in direct proportion to the effort put into the use and development of it.

If there is a double Life line on both hands, the person will be both spiritual and mediumistic especially if one of the lines is sitting on the mount of Venus. This person can become a channeler and be able to contact family members who have passed on.

Spirituality in the palms is often indicated by many fine spidery lines. Within these lies a deep well of understanding and sensitivity towards other people. This is created by a telepathic connection. If, by any strange chance, your partner also has the Mystic Cross in the quadrangle of the hand, you might wonder if he/she is your soul mate.

Finally, if there is a very large Cross in the quadrangle, not only is there a great amount of spirituality, the owner of this Cross is endowed with powerful healing ability.

Are You a Mystical Person?

The difference between the two previous types of people is that the mystical person looks beyond the psychic and spiritual energies which they have already worked through. Now they are looking inward for further truth and transforming experience within the ethereal light to become One with the Universe. They know that when they have had even just one mystical experience of the intense energy of the Universe and the love it contains, that the transformation and their own further evolution is starting in a totally different way – from a different viewpoint.

They know that their hard work and application over the years of employing

the Universal energy to themselves on a dedicated daily basis they have stepped upon the ladder of mysticism in expectation of more mystical experiences. So how do we know if a person is leaning in this mystical direction?

The key is the Ring of Solomon to be found on the base of the Index finger. It is a semi-circle around the base of the finger of Jupiter moving down towards the beginning of the Life line indicating a deep interest in the occult, showing that there is much talent in the use of psychic and universal powers. The Ring of Solomon is the master, the true adept compared to the Mystic Cross which is still in training, but both may well be found on the hand at the same time. The Ring of Solomon is the Wisdom of the Master, fully proficient in the use of Universal Energy, provided the ability to study and persevere has shown up in other areas of the hand. If not, these people who have these interests will indulge in idle chatter with little true knowledge and continue to dream their dreams of becoming a Master.

People who have achieved a status of applicable knowledge in either the psychic or spiritual worlds usually have spatulate or square finger tips and knotty finger joints. The mystical people tend to have the philosophical hand, the long, angular palm with bony fingers. They seek wisdom rather than wealth – it is the wealth of knowledge that they are after. These are the visionaries, the deep thinkers, silent and secretive, the Yogis, the church Cardinals, the Jesuits and many others.

Look now at the line of the Head. If it turns at the end sending an offshoot to the mount of the Moon this brings out the mystical inclination and the leaning towards knowing of the mysterious and hidden powers of the Universe. Within this particular aspect of the Head line and the Moon mount, they are capable of experiencing the light and energy around trees, plants, animals, and people and becoming aware of the impact of the auras of other people. This brings home the understanding that we are all One, we are all connected.

At the bottom of the palm, just above the wrist is the mount of Neptune. This is the connecting energy link between our outer and inner selves – the conscious and unconscious. Neptune is also the bridge between the mounts of the Moon and Venus. We know that Venus represents love, but not, in this case, the material love of possessions and money. This is the Heart Chakra of pure love energy. Neptune in astrology represents the higher spiritual octave of Venus.

The combination of the Moon, Neptune, and Venus produces a very mystical person who lives within the love energy of the Universe, for that is all that the Universe contains and it wraps us within it every moment of our existence. It is we, with our thoughts, who push it away, ignore it, or use our thoughts and minds in a negative hateful fashion. Joining this trio is the line of Mercury.

These are where our thoughts come from. By capturing them as they make the connection to the Moon, Neptune, and Venus, they bring the ideas and the information for our next step on both our worldly and inner paths. We feel these as hunches – intuition – that should be heeded for they take us onto the next step of connection.

The mount of Pluto connects with this enigmatic and mystically inclined group. It is found at the lower center of the palm where it meets the wrist, not far from the Neptune mount. Pluto represents change and transformation whether material or spiritual in origin. Even though you are mystically inclined, you will still have to deal with the triumphs and failures of the material world, relations with siblings that are challenging or needing to be changed, or the destruction and rebuilding of your lifestyle. Pluto deals with all this when lines from any or all of this group join up with it. This also includes making you look inside yourself when you feel the material world is too close – perhaps to physically heal yourself or maybe just psychically because you have picked up negative energy. The transformation that Pluto brings when this energy pattern is triggered in meditation can bring astounding mystical experiences and also bring karmic connections to your inner mind through both meditation and dreams.

The other interesting mount on the hand dealing more with spirituality than mystical is the mount of Uranus found where the Head line dips down to the mount of the Moon. If you draw all these mounts on a piece of paper you will see that they make a half circle – like the letter C, then add the Mercury line across to join them. Now add branch lines from Mercury pointing to all these mounts and you can see how thoughts from Mercury can inspire all the mounts and Uranus particularly.

A mystically inclined Uranian type who is endowed with the logic of Mercury and the idealism of Neptune will want to get involved with trying to raise mass consciousness to a spiritual level. Uranus deals with groups of people bringing inventive ideas into mind training, meditation devices, workshops, anything that will bring the mind of the people into the realm of Universal Consciousness. Along with Neptune's imagery, the Moon's inspiration, Venus love of beauty and humanity, bringing together a union between people or organizations of like minds both mystical and spiritual, all things eventually come together opening up the path to Mysticism and the most wonderful secrets of Universal Mind.

The After Word

Within these pages we have traveled the route from the material to the spiritual then to the mystical, deciding who we were before and what we have become now.

It's a fascinating journey of wonder and joy in uncovering yourself as a person you have never known before with talents and creativity you didn't know you had. As the Pluto mount suggests, transformation will definitely take place as the new person you have discovered takes shape.

I trust you will enjoy working with this book as much as I have enjoyed writing it. Even if you do not become a professional palmist, you will be enchanted with the new person you have grown to be.

~Maiya

Bibliography

Anderson Mary Palmistry. *Your Destiny in your Hands*. Weiser. New York, NY 1973

Benham William. *The Laws of Scientific Hand Reading*. Duall, Sloan and Pearce, NY, New York, 1966

Cheiro. *Cheiro's Language of the Hand*. Arc Books Inc. New York, NY 1968.

Gettings Fred. *The Book of the Hand*. The Hamlyn Publishing Group. Middlesex, England 1968

Gray-Cobb Geof. Illustrations from The Palmistry Workshop 1978

INDEX